SEED FOR THE SOWER
A N D
BREAD FOR THE EATER

YOU ARE VALUABLE AND PRECIOUS MY FRIEND

JERRY JACOB

WESTBOW
PRESS®
A DIVISION OF THOMAS NELSON
& ZONDERVAN

WestBow Press books may be ordered through booksellers or by contacting:

WestBow Press
A Division of Thomas Nelson & Zondervan
1663 Liberty Drive
Bloomington, IN 47403
www.westbowpress.com
844-714-3454

ISBN: 979-8-3850-3702-5 (sc)
ISBN: 979-8-3850-3703-2 (e)

Library of Congress Control Number: 2024922520

Print information available on the last page.

WestBow Press rev. date: 11/19/2024

GOD IS MOST GLORIFIED IN YOU WHEN YOU ARE MOST SATISFIED IN HIM. THE MEASURE OF GOD'S GLORY IS THE MEASURE OF YOUR SATISFACTION IN HIM. THERE IS A JOY YOU GET OUT OF THIS TRUST AND SATISFACTION. CHERISH THIS JOY IN YOUR LIFE JOURNEY THAT REMAINS NOT JUST FOR 80 OR 90 SCORES OF YEARS, BUT BEYOND - TILL ETERNITY!

YOUR SATISFACTION FOR THE BIGGEST AND LONGEST HAPPINESS IN LIFE, WOULD NOT BE AT ODDS WITH GOD'S WILL FOR YOUR LIFE. THEN YOUR HAPPINESS DOES NOT COMPETE WITH GOD'S GLORY. IN FACT, THEY WILL GO TOGETHER AND COMPLETE YOU WITH EVERLASTING JOY.

JESUS REPLIED: "LOVE THE LORD YOUR GOD WITH ALL YOUR HEART AND WITH ALL YOUR SOUL AND WITH ALL YOUR MIND.' THIS IS THE FIRST AND GREATEST COMMANDMENT AND THE SECOND IS LIKE IT: 'LOVE YOUR NEIGHBOR AS YOURSELF.' ALL THE LAW AND THE PROPHETS HANG ON THESE TWO COMMANDMENTS."

Acknowledgements

The compiler and writer takes permission in acknowledging, the kindness of the authors and publishers, to extract from their copyright publications. Indulgence is begged in case of failure to reach any author, or holder of copyrighted selections.

I am deeply grateful for the mercy and grace that God has bestowed upon me throughout this writing journey. The burden of God is translated to seek and bring home that painful soul into an eternal hope and joy.

I am thankful to my wife Sobha for her invaluable partnership and support throughout this writing process. Thanks to all the great men who inspired and shared this witness of the Light. I want to thank my two sons Joshua and Nethen, Parents, family and friends for all support and love. I extend my gratitude to Wesbow Printing for their role in bringing this book to publication.

Foreword

My heart extends to every friend around the world, inviting all to share in the joy of fellowship and triumph in life, regardless of our current circumstances. Whether you are bedridden for years, imprisoned, or bearing the weight of life's challenges, I earnestly pray that the truth shared, may invade the Atacama Desert of your dehydrated, empty and parched hearts. May it flow like a mighty river, bringing freshness, healing, and life. May this reading bless you to reign in life through the embodiment of truth.

A journey spanning years of collections and captured messages, carefully gathered and guided by God' Spirit for those who earnestly seek light and truth. The gaps I tried to fill in my own heart are now scripted in printed letters. It is written not to assert that truth is my exclusive inheritance, but to extend a hand to all nations and races—believer, unbeliever and every soul—with boundless love and camaraderie.

This book encapsulates few years of seeking, reading, curating collections, and scribbling messages. Its purpose is to unveil truths that resonate deeply with our essence and the reality we inhabit. My effort was to research and organize the information in a clear and structured manner. Truth relayed in the form of question and answers. Notes scribbled at different times, intended to share God's wisdom for inspiring hope, joy, and strength. Testimonies that partner with truth espouses like an aromatic chamomile flower.

Jesus did not claim to be a truth or to merely speak the truth; He declared, "I am the truth." This profound statement suggests that He was affirming His role as the source, final authority, and embodiment of Truth. That statement, definitely percolates our understanding, in such a manner that, it deploys us into a pursuit of the very nature of 'Truth'. Thus Truth is not merely a concept or a collection of facts, it is the essence of what God is. Jesus answers every question that we could have. "Why am I here?" ; "Who created this world?" ; "What is the purpose of everything?" ; "How does everything in the universe hold together?"; Is Jesus the truth of all God's promises?

Jesus answered, *"I am the way and the truth and the life. No one comes to the Father except through me."*(John 14:6). The terms "the way," "the truth," and "the life" have implications on your life in this present world and for eternity.

Please do not approach the biblical verses in this book assuming that, just because something is older, it must be outdated or less valuable. That way, we often overlook the context and complexity of historical truth, ideas or accomplishments.

Using our own worldview as a lens to examine other perspectives is like a biology student asking a physics teacher, "What is the Genetic code of Gravity?" I encourage readers to adopt a fresh perspective as they begin reading, setting aside preconceived opinions and viewpoints. A world view that merely answers intellectually is insufficient, it must also meet us existentially in our life.

Imagine a water fountain in the middle of a pool, where concentric rings of water ripple outwards from the center. As you move from the outermost ring toward the innermost circle near the fountain, you transition from relatively calm water to increasingly energetic and lively water. The closer you get to the fountain, the more vibrant and dynamic the water becomes. The chapters of this book have been arranged in a similar manner. Starting from the outermost ring, each chapter moving forward brings you closer to the heart of the fountain. As you progress through the chapters, you will experience a gradual increase in energy and life. Let nothing hinder your reading journey. I encourage you to read with this imagery in mind, moving inward until you reach the innermost ring near the fountain, where the book reaches its culmination. My hope is that, by the end, you will feel the profound energy and life that the fountain of God can bring, enlightening your soul with His divine light.

Compiled and written by Jerry Jacob.

Book Title Reflection

2 Corinthians 9:10 – *"He who supplies seed to the sower and bread for food will supply and multiply your seed for sowing and increase the harvest of your righteousness."*

Sowing and Harvesting represents the cycle of growth and fruition in human life. Sowing and Harvesting involves work. But we all work for the seed and bread that perishes eventually. Our hunger and thirst are the reasons that we have to work for it. Human effort is essential throughout the entire process of sowing and harvesting. But every human work does not always end in the fruit we expect. There are lot of external environmental factors like rain, snow and soil which affect growth and fruition.

This verse reveals that the God who gives life to the physical and natural world is also the One who will multiply that precious life cycle with righteousness until eternity. God provides the seed and bread that endures eternally. Hold this verse as a steadfast promise for your life until you meet the One who gave this promise.

What must we do, to be doing the works of God?

God says, with human effort we can neither sow nor harvest the eternally enduring true seed and bread. It is impossible for man. The seed and bread sent from heaven is dedicated solely to carry out God's eternal purpose and will. Different faith traditions and interpretations may offer specific insights into what constitutes God's will. We are going to read a passage, where Jesus reveals the will of God with clarity.

There is so much of injustice, pain and suffering around us. And human heart says, this temporal life is not sufficient enough for me, I need to live eternally in the fullness of life. Is it possible to have this eternal fullness? Jesus was once asked the same question. Though He answered, some grumbled. As the growth and fruition of seed depend on numerous factors, Jesus says, it is God who needs to grant access to this eternal seed and fruit. It is by identifying the true seed and true bread which God had sent. But the main issue our generation face, is the way we approach God. God is not a human in flesh and blood. He exists in a different realm which is eternal. God is a Spirit as we know from Jesus.

The increase in global connectivity has exposed many people to a variety of religious beliefs and practices, leading to a more pluralistic approach to spirituality. This is where we make the first wrong step. Or we approach God as we would any other human being, with a casual attitude, humanizing Him with a sense of equality and familiarity. There might be a concern, that approaching God in a human-like manner reduces the sense of mystery and wonder. Some approaches involve self- mutilation, fasting, and endless cycles of religious rituals and practices. Most of the time, we approach God for our wish list and needs required for our earthly existence. However, all these attempts raise a Red flag at times !!

Let us understand that God is an eternal, uncaused being, the Creator.

God simply is!

We are His creation. He does not need anything from us for His existence. We need to understand that creation is merely one of the wise thoughts of the Creator brought into existence, manifested into reality. This Creator has created everything for a reason, purpose with all complexity and precision. Precision and creativity must always be **accurate and truthful** because it maintains the integrity of the creating process, fostering trust and credibility of the final product. Truth and Integrity is one of the key attributes of a Creator.

When the crowd sought Jesus to witness God's work and asked for the bread that endures eternally, Jesus replied that they were seeking earthly satisfaction for their physical bodies. Red flag !! Jesus made it clear that their true intention was not seeking the truth. Our approach to God should be marked by honesty and a genuine desire to know Him, rather than focusing on what we can gain from Him. Jesus taught that entering the kingdom of God requires the innocence and openness of a child. God's communication is based on His two essential qualities: Truth and Spirit. By Spirit, I refer to the nature of Divine uniqueness and purity (God's Holiness), which we understand through His own Words. ***When approaching God, it is essential to come with both Truth and spiritual integrity as well.***

John 4:24, *"God is a Spirit: and they that worship Him must worship Him in spirit and in truth."*

I encourage you to reflect on the following passage depicting the interactions between the crowd and Jesus. Following Jesus' miracle of feeding five thousand people, the below passage continues with Jesus mentioning their ancestor Moses, whom they revered as a prophet of God and who had witnessed miracles nearly 1500 years before. It is a profound passage that reveals, how our human understanding and intentions does not align with God's perspective.

John 6:25-48, *NKJV "When they found Him on the other side of the sea, they said to Him, "Rabbi, when did you come here?" Jesus answered them and said, "Most assuredly, I say to you, you seek Me, not because you saw the signs, but because you ate of the loaves and were filled. Do not labor for the food which perishes, but for the food which endures to everlasting life, which the Son of Man will give you, because God the Father has set His seal on Him." Then they said to Him, "What shall we do, that we may work the works of God?" Jesus answered and said to them, "This is the work of God, that you believe in Him whom He sent." Therefore they said to Him, "What sign will You perform then, that we may see it and believe You? What work will You do? Our fathers ate the manna in the desert; as it is written, 'He gave them bread from heaven to eat.'" Then Jesus said to them, "Most assuredly, I say to you, Moses did not give you the bread from heaven, but My Father gives you the true bread from heaven. For the bread of God is He who comes down from heaven and gives life to the world." Then they said to Him, "Lord, give us this bread always." And Jesus said to them, "I am the bread of life. He who comes to Me shall never hunger, and he who believes in Me shall never thirst. But I said to you that you have seen Me and yet do not believe. All that the Father gives Me will come to Me, and the one who comes to Me I will by no means cast out. For I have come down from heaven, not to do My own will, but the will of Him who sent Me. This is the will of the Father who sent Me, that of all He has given Me I should lose nothing, but should raise it up at the last day. And this is the will of Him who sent Me, that everyone who sees the Son and believes in Him may have everlasting life; and I will raise him up at the last day."*

The Jews then complained about Him, because He said, "I am the bread which came down from heaven." And they said, "Is not this Jesus, the son of Joseph, whose father and mother we know? How is it then that He says, 'I have come down from heaven'?"

Jesus therefore answered and said to them, "Do not murmur among yourselves. No one can come to Me unless the Father who sent Me draws him; and I will raise him up at the last day. It is written in the prophets, 'And they shall all be taught by God.' Therefore everyone who has heard and learned from the Father comes to Me. Not that anyone has seen the Father, except He who is from God; He has seen the Father. Most assuredly, I say to you, he who believes in Me has everlasting life. **I am the bread of life."**

All the prophets and the books of Moses had spoken about God Who would be amongst man, providing them the bread for eternal life. Eternal words of life. God offers the everlasting seed and nourishment that can elevate us from our temporary existence to an eternal life, allowing our spirit, soul, and body to thrive in the imputed righteousness of God with confidence. *"The fruit of that righteousness will be peace; its effect will be quietness and confidence forever"* (Isaiah 32: 17,NIV).

Identifying the true bread from heaven is crucial in our spiritual journey. Isn't it wise to dedicate our time and resources to what is eternal and nourishing? Just as rain and snow fall from above to fulfill their purpose by nourishing seeds and eventually producing bread and fruit, nature teaches us how God works. He sends His true bread—the Word of God—from above, fulfilling His purpose by revitalizing our dry souls with the eternal springs of life-giving words from God Himself. In fact, the prophet Isaiah conveyed this same message over 600 years before Christ.

Isaiah 55:2-3,10-11, *"Why do you spend your money for that which is not bread, and your labor for that which does not satisfy? Listen diligently to me, and eat what is good, and delight yourselves in rich food. Incline your ear, and come to me; hear, that your soul may live; and I will make with you an everlasting covenant. For as the rain and the snow come down from heaven and do not return there but water the earth, making it bring forth and sprout, giving seed to the sower and bread to the eater, 1 so shall my word be that goes out from my mouth; it shall not return to me empty, but it shall accomplish that which I purpose, and shall succeed in the thing for which I sent it."*

This flourishing does not begin after our last breath and passing, but from the moment we believe in the True Bread sent by God. 'It calls us to believe in the One, God sent.' The work of God is to believe in His Son Jesus and through Jesus we receive the will of God - which is eternal life. This statement creates many a murmur. My sincere and humble endeavour is to collect all these murmurs, blend them with a unifying note, and turn them into an audible, humble symphony. God willing!

Contents

Chapter 1

A Note to My Friends and Brethren

Hello to all my friends, brothers, and sisters!

Firstly, I want to acknowledge and respect your perspective as an atheist or whatever world view or religion you may hold. I understand that we all have different worldviews, and that's perfectly okay. Our differences in beliefs should not hinder us from engaging in meaningful conversations and building bridges of understanding.

One of the core teachings of Christianity is love, compassion, and empathy. I believe that these values are universal and can be shared regardless of our beliefs. In that spirit, I approach this note with an open heart and a desire to connect on a human level.

Ultimately, my goal is not to convert or convince, but rather to foster understanding, empathy, and friendship. I believe that by seeking common ground and embracing our differences, we can build a more compassionate and inclusive world.

It saddens me to see some of my friends distance themselves from God when faced with overwhelming pain, loss, or situations beyond their control. My heart deeply empathizes with them. I am motivated to share the blessings and goodness I have experienced from God with my fellow brothers and sisters, hoping they too can become recipients and conduits of this goodness.

For many of my atheist friends and other world views, their worldview is not one of hopelessness, condemnation or despair but rather one of embracing life and finding meaning in human connections, morality, and the pursuit of knowledge. They often derive comfort from the idea that this life is the one we have, so it is essential to make the most of it and cherish the moments we have with loved ones. I understand that part and agree with it to an extend. But I want to make a meaningful conversation, finding common ground in shared experiences of loss. Showing kindness and understanding can bridge differences and strengthen relationships. Death and loss can be incredibly challenging and deeply impactful experiences for everyone. In Christ, we could find Hope in hopelessness, Joy in despair, Redemption in the midst of condemnation. If I have experienced it, won't that be a good if I can share with my fellow men? Isn't it difficult to bear such heavy burdens and pain? The depth of sorrow intensifies when someone passes away. I wish for my friends to experience lighter burdens and embrace the freedom, truth, and life found in Christ.

'As I walk past evening dusk, dark clouds, darker skies and storms, Yet nothing close to the darkness in our hearts,

Evil and weakness in our own empty hearts,

The darkness of nature's evil, nothing close to the evil in our own empty hearts. But yea, the rainbow that He promised, keeps shining in the midst of the storm.'

Universal setting of our empty hearts always traverses towards evil and disorder. The enlightened Paul even said, *"What a wretched man I am! Who will rescue me from this body of death?"*

Law of entropy from order to disorder is what my empty heart craves for. *"The heart is deceitful above all things and beyond cure. Who can understand it?"* says prophet Jeremiah17:9,NIV. We do not have to explain to a small child how to become stubborn or rebellious, he has an inherent sinful nature.

The fallen nature of man, is a reality of human heart. God has given us a choice of free will. He does not want us to become like automatons, androids or robots. It is in a free will natured condition that we experience all love, happiness, glory, hope, faith, redemption, relationships, evil, pain and also suffering.

Understanding someone else's suffering or pain is not easy unless we experience it first hand. External comments or opinions cannot truly grasp the depth of suffering. No scientific explanation can fully capture the truth of the situation—it is either an inadequate view or an overly critical analysis that does not offer real understanding to the person in pain.

Why do some people experience profound pain and suffering? Each person's life journey is unique, and they may face challenges or traumas that profoundly impact them. These could include loss, illness, abuse, or other personal struggles that shake their sense of well-being. Systemic issues like racism, sexism, or economic disparities cause pain. Some people grapple with existential questions about the nature of life, death, meaning, and purpose. These philosophical and spiritual inquiries can lead to deep emotional pain and existential crisis. Life can be unpredictable, and sudden events like accidents, natural disasters, or unexpected losses, conditions like fears, fear of death, depression, anxiety, or chronic pain can lead to profound suffering.

I know an aunt who had been battling Parkinson's disease for over six years. The progression of the illness had gradually restricted her movements, prompting modifications to her entire home to accommodate her needs. Six years ago, she could communicate and engage with us, with ease. Initially, she relied on support to walk around, eventually transitioning to a motorized wheelchair for mobility indoors.

Over time, even that became insufficient, and she spent most of her time in a specially designed bed that adjusts pneumatically to support her lying positions. A new machine was installed to assist her in case of falls or when she needs to be moved within the house. Three caregivers were dedicated to her care. Unfortunately, her ability to interact had weakened significantly.

Over time, her speech became restricted to a few words, each uttered with considerable effort. She easily became exhausted and fatigued. Despite medical attention, there remained a mysterious aspect to her condition that doctors could not fully explain. We remember her as a vibrant, positive individual, always eager to engage with others and full of energy beans during her healthier days. She is no more. It was several years of pain and trials.

All of us have enough intense stories to mention about our trials and pains. Where is my God?

"Terrors are turned upon me; my honor is pursued as by the wind, and my prosperity has passed away like a cloud.
"And now my soul is poured out within me; days of affliction have taken hold of me.
The night racks my bones, and the pain that gnaws me takes no rest.
With great force my garment is disfigured; it binds me about like the collar of my tunic.
God has cast me into the mire, and I have become like dust and ashes.
I cry to you for help and you do not answer me; I stand, and you only look at me.
You have turned cruel to me; with the might of your hand you persecute me. You lift me up on the wind; you make me ride on it, and you toss me about in the roar of the storm.
But when I hoped for good, evil came, and when I waited for light, darkness came.
My inward parts are in turmoil and never still; days of affliction come to meet me.
I go about darkened, but not by the sun; I stand up in the assembly and cry for help.

I am a brother of jackals and a companion of ostriches.
My skin turns black and falls from me, and my bones burn with heat.
My lyre is turned to mourning, and my pipe to the voice of those who weep."

This was quoted by none other than, a character named Job in the bible, Job Chapter 30:15-31. He lost his wealth, ten children, family and all reputation. The character Job we know suffered in all areas of his livelihood. Job who once was the wealthiest, powerful, God fearing man, inheritor of abundant spiritual and earthly blessings. God said there is none like him on earth. He was robbed of his wealth, fame, his ten children and their families overnight. He was knocked of his living daylights, that he was even forsaken by his wife and she probed him to slacken his own integrity and curse God. His whole body was filled with loathsome sores from the sole of his foot to the crown of his head. And he took a piece of broken pottery with which to scrape himself while he sat in the ashes. *"My flesh is clothed with worms and dirt, my skin hardens, then breaks out afresh."* (Job 7: 5). His friends seasoned his pain with liturgical notes of condemnation, judgements and accusations against him. He was bombarded in all dimensions of flesh, mind and spirit.

Job asked God, *"Why did you bring me out from the womb? Would that I had died before any eye had seen me and were as though I had not been, carried from the womb to the grave. Are not my days few? Then cease, and leave me alone, that I may find a little cheer before I go— and I shall not return— to the land of darkness and deep shadow, the land of gloom like thick darkness, like deep shadow without any order, where light is as thick darkness."* (Job10:18-22).

Where is God?

But why is God at times very silent during suffering of very small innocent baby or a life long bed ridden man or even a believer? Is God sadistic?

Why do you think Job, out of everyone, was chosen to go through such intense suffering? It is because there is a divine purpose in suffering that surpasses human comprehension. Accepting this can be challenging; Job's wife and friends could not grasp it. They struggled to understand or make sense of what they saw. Even Job, known for his wisdom and righteousness, was at a loss and could not fully grasp the situation. He tried to use his wisdom to explain it but found himself drained and struggling to understand God's will. Total meaninglessness filled his mind.

Job indeed holds a special place in the Bible as a figure chosen by God for a particular purpose. His story illuminates various aspects of God's will, such as testing faith, revealing human resilience, and showcasing the complexities of life's challenges. The Book of Job is not just a narrative but a profound wisdom book that reflects the realities of pain, suffering, and human condition. It provides a framework for us to relate our own experiences of adversity and find meaning within them.

Notice what Job says about his suffering.

Job 36:15, *"He delivers the afflicted by their affliction and opens their ear by adversity."*

Let us not look at the affliction as a problem.

God is going to bring us out of this Affliction by the Affliction itself.

Psalms 119:75, "I know, O Lord, that your rules are righteous, and that in faithfulness you have afflicted me."

Affliction is a package whose contents are God's faithfulness, His steadfast love and favour. The Cross of Jesus came with God's faithfulness, His steadfast love and favour. Christ overcame **death** through His own **death**. He overcame **Affliction** through His **Affliction**. It may sound absurd, but there is deep truth in it.

Why did Jesus suffer?

To attain perfection. To be crowned with glory and to lead many sons to Glory. Hebrews 2:9-11, *"But we see him who for a little while was made lower than the angels, namely Jesus, crowned with glory and honor because of the suffering of death, so that by the grace of God he might* **taste death for everyone***. For it was fitting that he, for whom and by whom all things exist, in bringing many sons to glory, should make the founder of their salvation* **perfect through suffering***. For he who sanctifies and those who are sanctified all have one source. That is why he is not ashamed to call them brothers."*

God wants to remove our imperfections and to share His glory.

For a child swimming for the first time the water is his biggest problem and he believes that water's sinking nature is for his destruction. The water becomes a threat to his Life and Being. Fearing it, could lead to the harm or even drowning. He needs to go through several days of fear in the water itself. But finally when he learns that the same water has a superior floating buoyant nature, his attitude about water changes. Similarly with sufferings or any harassment, during the course of suffering our imperfections change to perfections.

Water suddenly becomes a tool instead of being a problem. An eternal perspective is required when we look at our sufferings.

The development and maturation of large militaries, armed forces, and air forces are not quick processes. They require years of hard work, dedication, and facing various challenges and afflictions along the way. We know fever or pain is body's way of strengthening itself to fight off bacteria and illness. Pain can be God's invitation to live.

There is transfer of power during the course of suffering. Paul prayed three times to remove his physical infirmity but God chose to take him through it with His grace.

2 Corinthians12:9-10, *"But He said to me, "My grace is sufficient for you, for My power is made perfect in weakness." Therefore I will boast all the more gladly about my weaknesses, so that Christ's power may rest on me. That is why, for Christ's sake, I delight in weaknesses, in insults, in hardships, in persecutions, in difficulties. For when I am weak, then I am strong."*

There is a transfer of power from human effort to divine grace and strength. We also tend to think as humans, that we can display boldness and strength only when everthing goes well in and around us. But in God's kingdom His grace is sufficient in our weakness. God's grace is a word of promise from Him reaffirming that He is always with us and will never forsake us. And God's glory illuminates from us in our weakness.

1Peter 5:10, *"And after you have suffered a little while, the God of all grace, who has called you to his eternal glory in Christ, will himself **restore, confirm, strengthen, and establish** you."*

Suffering can be seen as a gift because it strips away false hopes. When all other sources of hope, such as money or health, fail us, suffering reveals that our only enduring hope lies in God. To hope in God is not a weakness. In fact, it is the first step to acknowledge His Holiness.

God is focused on developing the inner character and strength of individuals. No, it's not easy to go through the process of being molded, much like how gold is refined.

Romans 5: 2-5,NIV "And we boast in the hope of the glory of God. Not only so, but we also glory in our sufferings, because we know that <u>suffering produces</u> <u>perseverance</u>; <u>perseverance,</u> <u>character</u>; and <u>character, hope</u>. And hope does not put us to shame, because God's love has been poured out into our hearts through the Holy Spirit, who has been given to us."

A judge was once asked, Why do Tragedies happen? Why a loving God allow tragedies to happen?

The judge replied,

I asked God for strength and God gave me difficulties to make me strong

I asked for wisdom, God gave me problems to solve

I asked for courage, God gave me dangers to overcome.

I asked for love, God gave me troubled people to help.

My prayers were answered...

Our life on earth would be maximum 80 years or 90 years. But there is life beyond this earthly life to be spent in eternity where time is not measurable. From the creation of the first man until our current generation and generations which are yet to follow are all linked and have something in common. This common link is the "Will of God" which is being accomplished from generation to generation. We in our fraction of life within this long period of generations cannot even see, fathom God's purpose or will within our lifespan with our limited human wisdom. Imagine God's purpose for us in eternity, it is much beyond our understanding.

Daniel 12 : 2-3, *"And many of those who sleep in the dust of the earth shall awake, some to everlasting life, and some to shame and everlasting contempt. And those who are wise shall shine like the brightness of the sky above; and those who turn many to righteousness, like the stars forever and ever."*

Our wisdom falls short when it comes to fully comprehending the brilliance of brightness and the glory of stars. The total number of stars in the observable universe is estimated to be 1025 (1 followed by 25 zeros). Nobody knows the actual number. Today, the local Milky Way galaxy (of which our sun is a part) has been found to contain 200,000 million stars. What an astounding result! If somebody could count three stars per second, after 100 years he would have counted less than five percent of this number. What does the Bible say about the number of stars? Jeremiah writes: *"As the **host of heaven cannot be numbered**, neither the sand of the sea measured: so will I multiply the seed of David my servant."* (Jeremiah 33:22). Isaiah tells us that **God's thoughts and ways are far higher than ours** (Isaiah 55:8–9). Not only are His thoughts higher than ours, they are also much faster. He can count the stars! And He has done exactly that; ***He determines the number of the stars; he gives to all of them their names..***" (Psalm 147:4). The very next verse emphasizes His greatness: ***"Great is our Lord, and abundant in power; his understanding is beyond measure.***"

Heinz Kaminski, who was for many years director of the Bochum observatory, was once asked what his thoughts were when he first pointed his telescope at the heavens. He replied in Part: 4

'Astronomers have reduced man to an atomic nothing; he was continuously dragged out and left to stand alone like a worm at 17,000 million light-years. He is overwhelmed by the enormous stars and vast distances. To himself he appears tiny and insignificant. Clever people have forgotten that this puny human being occupies an important place in the eye of the Creator, as can be read in the Bible. When God had created the earth ... He then created man and gave him some crumbs of the greatness of His own Spirit. And these crumbs enable us to grasp something of the logistics of the entire system. If we did not carry this creative spark, we would not have been able to analyze the laws of the universe nor understand their effects.'

God is beyond our imagination, so the suffering or evil can be definitely linked to all this great plans of the Almighty. Paul says, 2Corinthians 4:*16-18*, *"So we do not lose heart. Though our outer self is wasting away, our inner self is being renewed day by day. For this light momentary affliction is preparing for us an eternal weight of glory beyond all comparison, as we look not to the things that are seen but to the things that are unseen. For the things that are seen are transient, but the things that are unseen are eternal."*

Many a times we limit, who God is, within our humanly wisdom. But God is someone beyond our thoughts and ways. Life has intense realities. Some of the painful realities is that there is no reconciliation in sight. When there is no reconciliation possible, we tend to reach many conclusions. Our notion of God lies in the below, it is a trilemma :-

God is all-powerful: He can do anything He wills.

God is all-loving: He cares with an intense value for His creation. Evil is a reality: Suffering is an all-pervading part of this world.

'If God is all powerful, why suffering?' is the bell which shudders our spirit of faith and understanding. Are you really there God?

C.S. Lewis - *'It is critically important to examine the assumptions within a question. Its an existentially felt question that often doesn't examine the logical presuppositions within this. God has to remain in the paradigm for the question to be real.'*

To understand this we need to have profound knowledge about the Holy One. We know, God is holy; holiness is something beyond morality, it is more than just doing right. It is more to do with the perfection of His goodness and being. It is the actual distance between man and God. More often we try to understand God within our human wisdom and experience. God's thoughts and ways are not like man's. He does not work and think the ways we prefer. We need to get this right, in the first place. Holiness is the fullness of God' persona which cannot be fully known or perceived by our physical existence.

We are entrenched by the glory of God in all the earth. *"Holy, holy, holy is the Lord of hosts; the whole earth is full of His glory!"* (Isaiah 6:3). God is holy and desires us to become holy .

Dr. R.C. Sproul says, **"The holiness of God affects every aspect of our lives— economics, politics, athletics, romance—everything with which we are involved."** For God to reveal His holiness the flesh body is never a barrier for His revelation. Even the cross was not a blockade to reveal this holiness. Where was God during the suffering of the Cross? God displays His holiness through divine wisdom.

Luke 8 : 16, *"No one lights a lamp and hides it in a clay jar or puts it under a bed. Instead, they put it on a stand, so that those who come in can see the light."*

God's wisdom appears to be foolishness for a man in the flesh, because our mind, traditions and learning has been acquainted and familiarized with generations of earthly wisdom, experience and our mind goes deep only as far as the sensitivity and wisdom of human mind. The brightest human minds is said to possess only 2% of knowledge from the vast human knowledge it preserves. Then how could he comprehend with God's wisdom. To comprehend God's wisdom, man needs to understand His overall design and sovereign plan. The design and plan we know about God is quite often constrained by us to our human flesh body requirements. For instance our physical health, livelihood, education, well being and every aspect of our physical needs. All the earthly blessing we receive for our physical existence from God is also part of this list. These eventually decay on a daily basis as we advance in years. God is a Spirit. He wants us to be His children in spirit. The glory we receive is for our inner man, the spirit. Suffering is precursor to a thing called " Gods Glory." We generally try to link our suffering in the physical to a loss or pain or sorrow. We assume it as atrocious, since we always carry a lot of worldly wisdom and have been educated about importance of our Physical existence all our lives. The value and the marks we put for it is always immense. We attribute all our existence to this being in our flesh body. But the only thing which remains eternal is our spirit man, which we do not have any wisdom about. To have wisdom about our spirit, the only source available is the Eternal Spirit called God. This wisdom about our spirit or inner man can be understood only from God. No other human definition will be truthful and accurate.

Romans 8:13-17, *"For if you live according to the flesh you will die, but if by the Spirit you put to death the deeds of the body, you will live. For all who are led by the Spirit of God are sons of God. For you did not receive the spirit of slavery to fall back into fear, but you have received the Spirit of adoption as sons, by whom we cry, "Abba! Father!" The Spirit himself bears witness with our spirit that we are children of God, and if children, then heirs—heirs of God and fellow heirs with Christ, provided we suffer with him in order that we may also be glorified with him."*

Pierre Teilhard de Chardin - *'We are not human beings having a spiritual experience. We are spiritual beings having a human experience.'*

God Himself has to teach us, on how to understand Him. For eg, Parents have to teach their baby, on how to talk, walk and behave like them. The child also needs to gain self-understanding while listening to what his parents say. In short the child should understand the language, plans and actions of his parents. Similarly, the Holy Spirit has to teach the human spirit about the ways of God. The Word of God are the ways of God. Psalms 119:105, *"Your word is a lamp to my feet and a light to my path."* It is the spirit in man which gives him insight and understanding. We quite often assume insight and understanding is only for the learned and aged. God's Spirit illuminates our spirit.

Proverbs 20:27, *"The spirit of man is the lamp of the Lord, searching all his innermost parts."*

Job 32:8-9, *"But it is the spirit in man, the breath of the Almighty, that makes him understand. It is not the old who are wise, nor the aged who understand what is right."*

We receive earthly and spiritual blessings from the Lord.

What are spiritual blessings? (Ephesians 1 indicates the below)

- – In Christ, we are blessed with every spiritual blessing in heavenly realms.
- – We are chosen, akin to being the chosen one like Jesus.
- – God views us as holy and blameless.
- – We are adopted as sons.
- – Through redemption, we are forgiven

- God's grace enriches us with wisdom and insight, akin to receiving direct light from Him.
- God reveals the mystery of His will to us, making us faithful partners.
- There's a unity between heaven and earth in us.
- We inherit eternal blessings.
- Our value is immeasurable; we cannot be scaled by human standards.
- We gain insight into God's purpose and the counsel of His will, shaping our eternal and powerful spiritual identity.
- Sealed with the Holy Spirit, we are declared righteous and destined for eternal life with God.
- We are enriched with faith, hope, and love.
- We are God's inheritance, reflecting our immense value in His eyes.

For now let us understand, God wants to bless us spiritually, they are those blessings meant for our human spirit (inner man) for us to be refined, in order to exist with a Holy God in His kingdom. The kingdom of God is wherever the Presence of God is.

Why does He want us to possess spiritual blessings, not just earthly physical blessings?

We often prioritize earthly blessings and overlook spiritual ones. When Jesus healed a sick man, he first granted a spiritual blessing by forgiving the man's sins before addressing his physical ailment. Jesus understood that spiritual blessings hold greater significance than physical healing. Jesus tells the lame, *"Now your sins are forgiven, take up your mat and walk."*

He recognized that our true battles are spiritual, as mentioned in Ephesians 6:12,NIV *"For our struggle is not against flesh and blood, but against the rulers, against the authorities, against the powers of this dark world and against the spiritual forces of evil in the heavenly realms."*

Perhaps we underestimate the importance of spiritual blessings. God desires us to share these blessings with others, as stated in 1Peter 3:9, *"Do not repay evil with evil or insult with insult. On the contrary, repay evil with blessing, because to this you were called so that you may inherit a blessing."*

God aims for us to reflect His likeness and ultimately be possessed by Him. Jesus exemplified spiritual sacrifice by rejecting His own desires and enduring suffering on the cross. God regards each of us as spiritual kings and priests, requiring training and wisdom to reach that level. Are you aware of this perspective? God's way of doing this depends on His specific purpose through you. It may involve suffering, pain.

The loving parent is not the one who never allows suffering in a child's life. The loving parent is the one who is willing to suffer alongside their children. If you have ever experienced deep depression or thought about dying, Jesus is right in front of you as a living example. There is no depth of agony and helplessness we can experience in this life that He does not understand. Jesus said to His friends, *"My soul is overwhelmed with sorrow, to the point of death."* (Matthew 26:38,NIV).

Think about it. He Himself had to go through immense pain, suffering, treachery, shame, torture, disdain, rejection, mental agony like each one of us.

How can God justify Himself if He does not know what men experience in this world. God had to experience Himself as a man through the man Jesus Christ, who was truly man and truly God.

After your death, when you stand in front of God, as a human, you could justify yourself and quote, 'God you are in Heaven, have you ever been here with me on the earth? Have you ever experienced the life of a human being and its pain?' But with Jesus as God, you cannot ask Him, those questions. Because, He has been through our pain and our suffering. The Bible says, *"that at the name of Jesus every knee should bow, in heaven and on earth and under the earth, and every tongue acknowledge that Jesus Christ is Lord, to the glory of God the Father."* Philippians 2:10-11,NIV

The Bible says that the eternal life that God offers to every person will be one where *"God will wipe every tear from our eyes,"* where there will be *"no more death or mourning or crying or pain."* (Revelation 21:4,NKJV).

I have a young friend in my neighborhood who grew up in a loving Christian family and was deeply involved in Sunday School until graduating high school. However, during college, he experienced the tragic loss of a close friend, which created a significant emotional distance from God. The pain of losing someone dear is indescribable and can shake our beliefs to the core.

I tell my young friend not to completely shut the door on his faith in God. It's crucial to keep a connection open, allowing God to work through the pain and sorrow. Closing off this connection can lead to feelings of despair and a loss of hope beyond this lifetime. We must train our minds to endure not just for our earthly years but also for eternity.

Child like faith plays a pivotal role here, as Jesus likened the kingdom of heaven to that of little child. Trusting in our Heavenly Father, Who promises to never abandon us, is key.

I encourage him to delve into the teachings of the Gospels and the Word of God, shifting focus from pain and logical reasoning to surrendering control to God.

I share with him the analogy that God has given him a staff, much like Moses had. With this staff, he can either command the Red Sea to part and confidently walk through it, or he can stand before the ocean, acknowledging its might and depth. Jesus chose to walk through the Red sea of His Cross.

The subject of suffering is very sensitive and a very weighty spiritual subject to be handled tenderly with care as the pain of the sufferer cannot be perceived or clearly grasped by any other third person, no matter how much wisdom we possess. Earthly wisdom truly cannot reveal the glory hidden in every suffering. But God's wisdom is revealed in the suffering which surpasses all human understanding about the situation.

Answering questions about suffering is not straightforward because it is a sensitive topic that touches on subjects of value. Its not at all easy to go through that, personally as each one of us has a lot to say about suffering..

The short answer is, " I don't know..."

But we always seek for a reliable answer with truth.

Suffering is always linked to value. We experience suffering because we recognize the worth of a person, regardless of who they are.

At some point the philosophical rubber meets the existential rubber. I agree. No logic or philosophy can answer the depth of pain and suffering. You need to have an answer which needs to be not only true but relevant.

Atheism does not have an answer. If there is no God, life is meaningless tragedies and meaningless good fortune. Death of your dear one is meaningless. The central question all world views ponder is, how do I escape the endless cycle of suffering?

Some quote, Suffering is an illusion and need to be free from it. Another says, we need to be free of desires. Yet another, asking us to dwell in the Power of Now.

Paradox is that, do we really think that suffering is an illusion ? If you lose your dear child or any dear one, is it still an illusion ? No ! truth is, we don't think it is an illusion. When you say your suffering was an illusion, you are saying, the dear person you lost is nothing. The moment called 'Now' is truly awful, because of the loss in the past and the hopelessness of the future. Suffering is the signal of value, we know it, as we lose someone special. In the midst of suffering, I find meaning in the cross of suffering, where Christ endured pain for both you and me. The suffering which led to an eternal hope for all humanity unto eternal life.

Suffering arises from the free will choices we make in this fallen world.

When Man was first created, he was in union with God. There was no sin to separate him from His Creator. Whether you view the first three chapters of Genesis as an actual, historical account of events or a metaphorical concept of the creation and the Fall, in either case there was a time during which Man and God were in a relationship that involved no sin and then there was a time at which Man sinned and was separated from God.

This separation is named as the **Fall of man**. Fall into sin. A condition of separation from God. Free will choice is a blessing God has given us, so that we can Love each other. Love cannot be expressed without free will. Yet, it comes at the expense of suffering, as we often describe darkness as the absence of light.

I find it challenging to address this sensitive subject in a manner that can resonate with all perspectives or world views, as truth tends to be exclusive. Please forgive me for any shortcomings in my response.

God's allowance of suffering for a greater purpose is a concept that spans various religions such as Islam, Judaism, Hinduism, Buddhism, and Christianity. While it is acknowledged as a theory, it may not inherently bring comfort to us. However, for a Christ follower like me, it is more than theory because, in history, God did allow suffering with His own Son on a cross for the greatest possible good of salvation. This sacrificial act extends to everyone, including those who have passed away, offering redemption. It was indeed a wrathful suffering Christ endured.

Value of something depends on how much you are willing to pay for it. Imagine your house is on fire..we would risk to any extent to get our dear ones out of it, in the first instance. If we go by the logic of a blind pitiless mindless world view of a secular humanist, where man is a machine as a result of chemical process ..... should never care or would never pay for you...Honest Atheism world view does not add value or meaning to your existence. Yet we do care, nurture, value and love because we were wired into a relationship and bonding prototype of our Creator, which is the signature of our human minds created by even a superior mind of God..... The God who created you and your dear ones values you so much immeasurably because an <u>immeasurable God</u> pays an <u>immeasurable price</u> to spend an <u>immeasurable eternity</u> with you and me. All dots get connected only if we understand God and his triune nature. The relationship and bonding nature we acquire was originally from the relationship and bonding nature which existed within a triune God (Father, Son and Holy spirit).

I am concerned that we are still in a world where values have been distorted. The distinction between what is good and what is bad is highly relative across different perspectives. Sometimes, even the next generation can have a mixed-up understanding of these values. It is the consequence of our naturally deceitful hearts when people stray from the true light found in God. Lying seems to be an art form. Respecting elders is out of fashion. It is a poignant result of the inherent sin within humanity. The comforting aspect is that there is a God who reigns over all life's circumstances; we can rely on Him to bring about good from everything. Sin was conquered already on the cross through Christ Jesus, that all of us have been made, *"more than conquerors."* Which means that, now I do not have to fight a war against sin, it was already fought and won on the cross. All I need to do is trust in the One, God sent and receive the free gift of righteousness and salvation. But we have an inherent pride at different levels, that even we are not ready to receive something free from God. Our ego drives us to believe, that we must earn these gifts by our so-called good works, yet human righteousness falls short of the standards set by a Holy Holy Holy God Almighty.

Our own heart is the most deceitful thing in the world. It can deceive our thoughts, feelings, emotion. But then you say, then whom do I trust ? I trust then on the most reliable person, who carried no sin, whose words are words of eternal life and someone who has raised from death and has wisdom and knowledge about my own spirit, soul and body. That is why, I can relate to Jesus, God incarnated in flesh.. Isn't it the way we lead our life by always trusting on the most reliable thing available to us. We do not scientifically evaluate a woman before choosing her as a wife. If you try to experiment or test her extensively beforehand, she will likely feel hurt or betrayed. It is best not to experiment in such ways, or you might end up getting burned yourself. Many husbands can attest to this.

Without God, we cannot find objective meaning, purpose and stumble to find the right answers and conclusions. We would lack a foundation for knowing and understanding the world fully.

Existentialist philosophers like Jean-Paul Sartre, Viktor Frankl and Albert Camus have argued that life inherently lacks meaning, and it is up to individuals to create their own purpose. Sartre famously said, 'Existence precedes essence,' implying that humans must define their own essence through action. Human flourishing, Objectivity vs Subjectivity, Nature vs Nurture, Postmodernism and Nihilism - a more pessimistic viewpoint, posits that life is inherently meaningless and any search for inherent purpose or value is futile.

When we observe nature, God' creation, we do find meaning, purpose, and intelligent design. Jesus' teachings offer a framework for understanding meaning, purpose, and morality that centers on love for God and others, service, spiritual priorities, ethical living, forgiveness, and the pursuit of truth through a relationship with Him. In Matthew 6:19-21, Jesus advises, " *Do not lay up for yourselves treasures on earth, where moth and rust destroy and where thieves break in and steal, but lay up for yourselves treasures in heaven, where neither moth nor rust destroys and where thieves do not break in and steal. For where your treasure is, there your heart will be also.*" This suggests that true meaning and purpose are found in spiritual and eternal pursuits, rather than in the fleeting, material aspects of life, which only last for the brief span of 80 or 90 years. Jesus instills the hope of eternal life in our hearts, fulfilling the innate yearning of the human spirit.

Chapter 2

You Need Blind Faith to Become an Atheist

My intention is to first understand how we can connect our existence with the reality that surrounds us. It is important to emphasize the misconceptions and fallacies that often cloud our reasoning and observations. We get lost at times, because we make a false start and end up at the wrong landing position. Understanding these fundamental principles of logic and reality is crucial for us. I am striving to organize our thoughts systematically so that we can arrive at the truth and enhance our faith. We will delve into specifics in the upcoming chapters; let's begin with the key points,

- We cannot prove God, but we can have evidence and reason for God's existence. Proof is a fact that can demonstrate the truth. Evidence is information, we can trust leading to the truth. For example, no one can prove that George Washington was a real person but there is evidence in history that he existed and was the President of USA. That is how we live and build our daily lives, relying on evidence of truth.
- Nothing does not produce everything. Actually 'Nothing' produces nothing. Some Atheist believe that the whole universe was created from Nothing.
- Order and design points to a Designer with a mind. When we see order at our home, we know there is a mind that worked to get things in order.
- Universe is not eternal. It has a beginning. The Big Bang shows there is a beginning of time, space and matter. Universe was created by a timeless, spaceless and matterless uncaused cause, whom we define as God.
- Irreducible complexity points to a God. For eg, a cell, human eyes etc are complex and intelligently designed.
- Densely packed information always points to an Intelligent mind (DNA). Chaos cannot produce information. Complex designs can produce information.
- Unconscious cannot produce Conscious. A stone has no will, emotion and a mind. Our Human conscious mind cannot be produced by a primordial scum, mutation, lightning, evolution or chemical process.

- Innate drive for meaning and purpose in Life is only possible if there is a God (Camou paraphrases, *"that an honest atheist has to end in suicide."*). Atheists and secular thinkers find profound meaning and purpose in life through human connections, personal growth, contributing to society, and other intrinsic values. Existentialist philosophers like Jean-Paul Sartre and Albert Camus argued that individuals can create their own meaning and purpose in life through their choices and actions, even in a universe that may seem indifferent or devoid of inherent meaning. Camus, for instance, explored the concept of "absurdism," where the human search for meaning meets the silent, indifferent universe. Atheists' subjective meanings and purposes in life do not derive from a universe created from 'nothing' or from their understanding of human evolution from primordial origins and chemical processes. A stone or a chemical does not have a mind to provide meaning and purpose. It posits that atheists may need to draw upon elements of the theistic worldview to justify their perspectives on meaning and purpose. Existentialists have to lean upon and borrow from Theistic world views.
- Randomness cannot produce fine tuning. The Anthropic Principle is a philosophical and scientific concept that suggests the universe is finely tuned to allow for the existence of life, including human beings. It proposes that the fundamental constants and physical laws of the universe are precisely calibrated in a way that supports the emergence and sustenance of life as we know it. This idea is often discussed in the context of the "Goldilocks Zone," where conditions are just right for life to thrive, neither too hot nor too cold, neither too close to a star like the Sun nor too far away.
- Historical resurrection of Christ shows there is life after death, unlike an atheist for whom death is the final stop in life.
- Moral absolutes demands a moral law giver. Only God can give objective morality. All other morality which comes from men are relative. But our daily existence shows that, we cannot survive without having objective moralities. Rape of a small child is objectively evil. For an honest atheist, morality is always relative with each person. Atheist world view has no objective morality, good or evil is all relative. Murdering a Jew may be evil, but for a Nazi – it is good as per their atheistic world view. But we know that, it is not in line with the way we live, respond and think. Murdering a Jew or any human being is objectively evil.
- Non-life cannot produce life. Observing all plants, animals, man we know that life always comes from life. In our experience, life never comes from non-life.
- Love. Our experience of love says, there is more to reality than matter and energy. Caring for others. Love is not a chemical reaction and cannot be found

in blood samples. Love is intangible, nonphysical. Love is what makes the world go round..

- Reason cannot come from Non reason. A rational mind points to a Rational God. Observing Life and reality, we always find meaning and reason in life from a thinking mind.

These are intense, vast topics, you might find conflicting. We will get into the clarifications as we read on…

> "Modern man thought that when he had gotten rid of God, he had freed himself from all that repressed and stifled him. Instead, he discovered that in killing God, he had also killed himself. For if there is no God, then man's life becomes absurd."

Chapter 3

Rationality - Reason

If we can agree that the sky is blue, for example.. how is it that such an agreement is possible? If the world is a world of chance, how could anybody agree on anything? Agreement presupposes a world made by God, designed to be orderly and designed to be known by rational minds. It is a true knowledge that an unbeliever has, but suppresses a knowledge that he has in common with the believer. (Romans 1:21-25)

For example, he urges the apologist to show

"the non-Christian that even in his virtual negation of God, he is still really presupposing God." Clearly, when the unbeliever presupposes God in this sense, he is not acknowledging God as his ultimate commitment.

Assuming the intelligibility of the world, the unbeliever implicitly concedes the existence of the God that he explicitly denies. For the unbeliever to presuppose God in this context is for him to think, say, or do something, contrary to his own inclination, that indicates at some level of his consciousness a recognition of God's reality and significance.

The word presuppose is predicated not of persons, but of things: arguments, methods, knowledge, academic disciplines, affairs (such as the intelligibility of the universe). In such contexts, the word can be taken to mean "necessary conditions" or "that which legitimises".

If Some thing A presupposes B, then B is that to which a person must be committed if the person is to give an intelligible account of A. (Reasoning by presupposition or transcendental argument)

But it is important to remember that the rationality of which we speak, the rationality that serves as the rational basis for faith, is God's own rationality. The sequence is as follows:

God's rationality → human faith → human reasoning. The arrows may be read, "is the rational basis for."

So in this sense, the sequence is linear, not circular.

If faith aligns with God's truth, then it follows that genuine faith harmonizes with the highest forms of human reason, as our reasoning nature reflects God's image. Reason and faith are not in opposition but rather complementary. When we view reason as a gift from God, it becomes a means to understand His creation and the truths He reveals. God, as the source of all wisdom and understanding, imparts to us a capacity for reason that, when rightly directed, brings us closer to His truth. Faith helps us transcend the limitations of human understanding, guiding us into the mysteries of God that reason alone might not fully comprehend. Yet reason plays a crucial role by giving structure to our beliefs, enabling us to articulate, reflect upon, and share them in meaningful ways. This unity is beautifully reflected in figures like Augustine and Aquinas, who saw faith as illuminating reason and reason as deepening faith. God gave us our rational equipment not to deceive us, but so that we might gain knowledge, apart from sin, we may trust it to lead us into the truth; and even to sinners, the facts of God's creation bear clear witness of him to the human mind (Romans. 1:20).

In biblical argument, therefore, there is both reasoning and evidence; the clear revelation that God has given of Himself in the created world. So it is both right and proper to use evidences and human logic to confirm faith. Scripture does this very thing, frequently calling on people to the evidences of the truth (Psalm 19:1; Luke 1:1-4; John 20:30-31; Acts 1:1- 3; 26:26; Romans1:19-20). Biblical religion is unique in its appeal to history as the locus of divine revelation. God has plainly revealed Himself both in nature and in historical events.

When people say, 'You cannot use Scripture to prove Scripture conclusions?' --- Every philosophy must use its own standards in proving its conclusions; otherwise, it is simply inconsistent.

Rationality and faith can coexist in several ways. God created both the physical and spiritual world. There are physical and metaphysical realities which coexist. Rationality may be applied to empirical observations, scientific inquiry, and logical reasoning about the natural world, while faith may guide beliefs about existential questions, morality, and spiritual experiences transcend empirical verification. In different contexts, individuals may emphasize rationality or faith depending on the situation. Rationality and faith inform each other. We can question assumptions, examine evidence, and explore the implications of the beliefs, aiming to achieve coherence and understanding within the worldview.

Hebrews 11:1,NIV, *"Now faith is confidence in what we hope for and assurance about what we do not see."* This verse emphasizes that faith involves trust and confidence in things that are not immediately observable or provable through empirical evidence. It suggests that faith operates in a realm beyond mere rationality or empirical verification, focusing instead on assurance in beliefs that transcend physical evidence. While this verse highlights the aspect of faith, the Bible also encourages believers to use reason and understanding in their faith journey.

For instance, in Proverbs 2:6, it states: *"For the Lord gives wisdom; from His mouth come knowledge and understanding."* This verse suggests that knowledge and understanding are gifts from God, implying that rationality and the pursuit of wisdom are valued within the context of faith.

Faith, as mentioned in the Bible, is what grants victory over the world. This does not diminish the importance of reason or knowledge. It is not a blind faith that disregards facts. As St.Paul aptly pointed out, the historical resurrection of Jesus is the 'Reason for his Faith' in Christ. It is very clear in all parts of the scripture. The bible also acknowledges that human reason can change or evolve, depending on new findings and research.

Rationality alone cannot provide all answers. Over dependence on rationality is what we need to be careful about. Your own understanding can change. It can fall short. This verse in book of Proverbs encourages trust in God while acknowledging the limits of human understanding,

Proverbs 3:5-6, *"Trust in the Lord with all your heart, and do not lean on your own understanding. In all your ways acknowledge him, and he will make straight your paths."*

John 20:29, *"Jesus said to him, "Have you believed because you have seen me? Blessed are those who have not seen and yet have believed."*

This verse acknowledges the importance of faith even when physical evidence is not directly observable, highlighting the blessing of faith that goes beyond empirical proof.

Romans 1:20, " *For his invisible attributes, namely, his eternal power and divine nature, have been clearly perceived, ever since the creation of the world, in the things that have been made. So they are without excuse.*" This verse suggests that the natural world itself provides evidence of God's existence and attributes, implying a rational basis for belief in the divine. These verses reflect various aspects of how faith, reason, and knowledge interact within the biblical context, emphasizing both the importance of faith in God and the compatibility of faith with reasoned understanding and explanation.

Reason can also falter due to the corruption in this world caused by evil desires. History itself serves as ample evidence of this reality. We all face harsh realities in life, and sometimes it becomes difficult to accept what life throws at us. The storms of life can bring feelings of meaninglessness, causing us to lose our sense of rationale in the face of severe challenges.

In such dark times, reason often fails to provide any light or solace. This is a reality that each of us, including myself, have faced. Our dreams shatter and fall apart, and I have countless testimonies of my own. During such times, a scarlet blood-stained rope of hope was extended to me through the promises given by my Savior, Jesus Christ.

But God has divinely provided what ever we need for this life through the '**Promises**' He has given us, which is the **reason** that we can build up **Faith**. The faith we need is built on a reason, which is the foundation of God's promises. God's promises and His oath are unchanging. From Genesis to Revelation, we see God's promises. The way to receive these promises is through faith. Faith can overcome the corruption in this world. **Faith is made complete by adding goodness, knowledge of God, self-control, patience, godliness, mutual affection, and God's love**.

2 Peter 1: 3-8,NIV, "*His divine power has given us everything we need for a godly life through our knowledge of Him Who called us by His own glory and goodness. Through these He has given us His very great and precious promises, so that through them you may participate in the divine nature, having escaped the corruption in the world caused by evil desires. For this very reason, make every effort to add to your faith goodness; and to goodness, knowledge; and to knowledge, self-control; and to self-control, perseverance; and to perseverance, godliness; and to godliness, mutual affection; and to mutual affection, love. For if you possess these qualities in increasing measure, they will keep you from being ineffective and unproductive in your knowledge of our Lord Jesus Christ.*"

Faith and reason originate from a thinking mind bestowed upon us by God Himself, enabling us to thrive and contribute positively in a world tainted by corruption and evil.

Chapter 4
Truth Tests

When discussing different worldviews, it is crucial to ensure we are not asking self-defeating or self-contradictory questions. The questions we pose reflect back on us as questioners. If we abandon our discussions midway, we often find ourselves leaning towards either Pluralism or Atheism, possibly due to subjective reasons. Our close friend circle group discussions can often lead to humorously brushing off serious topics under the guise of peace and camaraderie, ending up with a diluted focus on lesser issues rather than tackling the main subject.

For instance, a conversation about God and humanity might meander into discussing empathy during social drinking, veering away from deeper philosophical considerations. We enjoy exploring diverse aspects of life as a spectator but often shy away from confronting them directly. Attempting to encapsulate complex subjects like reality, metaphysics, God, and humanity into one-liners or brief discussions only adds confusion without providing a lasting solution or deeper understanding.

In essence, our casual conversations can sometimes trivialize profound subjects, which is not a sustainable or effective approach to understanding them.

Mortimer Adler and his colleague Hutchins compiled an exceptional collection, the Great Books of the Western World program, spanning 55 volumes covering various subjects penned by eminent authors and thinkers throughout history. Within this collection, each subject, be it the universe, engineering, astrology, karma, or others, features insights and viewpoints from renowned experts and thinkers. Notably, the volume dedicated to the topic of God stands out with the most extensive content compared to other subjects.

Adler observed that among all the profound topics, the subject of God consistently elicits the greatest interest and concern from a diverse range of people.

Why does this topic hold such significance ? Does the concept of an unseen reality matter significantly to us ? And does this unseen reality exert a substantial influence on the visible world ? Analogously, just as the apple fruit is the primary purpose of an apple tree, despite the essential roles played by leaves, roots, soil, water, and minerals, could it be that humanity is the paramount goal of its Creator ? Every fruit, including the apple, carries the imprint of its Creator—the seed.

Essentially, Adler's observations prompt deeper reflections on the profound importance of exploring unseen realities and their potential impact on the visible world and human existence.

Do not get mesmerized by the esoteric words or folly which different authors or teachers or world views come up with. Some of them may sound sophiscated, mystical and vibrant, but may be hollow in its reality. Some of them may sound so pristine and make the other look horrific just like we see in political speeches. Brilliance need not be always the Truth. Try, not to be blown away by the mass marketing of spirituality. Search of Truth is your way to your Ultimate Reality. There is a need to ask the proper questions.

The best way of approaching is to vehemently and passionately search for the truth. But we do not take that route further, pursuing for the truth. As long as all our needs in this physical realms are met, we do not walk that extra yard. There is a seen and unseen reality. If we believe only in a seen reality, you are not a pragmatist neither a politician. Look at a small child, a farmer, a fisherman and a class teacher who can always envision an unseen reality in their respective fields. We may think we are clever enough to fool other people, God, or even ourselves, but little do we know of the ultimate consequences of our attempts to deceive reality.

However painful or awkward the truth may be, it is "truly" our only opportunity to create harmony and receive God's grace.

Any institution, country or even a small unit like a family cannot be peaceful and harmonious for a long time until it is embedded in Love. Love is not irritable or resentful; it does not rejoice at wrongdoing, but rejoices with the truth. In short, truth is mandatory in any situation in order to display and experience true love. Honestly speaking, we are not able to handle the Truth, because of our subjective reasons. We have lot of data and information about facts. But all facts need not be true.

To get straight to the point, it's the sin or darkness inside us, that we want to shy away from the Light of Truth. Strip away all veils of biases, including those related to caste, religion, tradition, location and any others, right from the start.

Truth by definition is exclusive. The moment you make an affirmation or an assertion about life' essence and meaning, you are implicitly saying that something that is contradictory to that is either false or your way is one way of thinking and it is not the truth. Law of non contradiction applies to realities, opposite things cannot be true. Truth is primarily a property of propositions. You see this in the court room. When you go to a court of law, you are always asked questions, with the attorney on the other side of the issue looking for two things >>Coherence and Correspondence.

Correspondence- applies to particular assertions and statements eg.., If the lawyer asks,"Where were you at the time of murder ?" If your answer was, "No I wasn't there at the place of murder." They will make sure that you say the truth, but yet that one answer does not mean that you have nothing to do with the murder, but it only says that you were not there at the time of murder.

Secondly, the lawyer will try to test you, not just on corresponding truth but coherence in all the truth statements you presented. Are all of your answers fitting together in a coherent response for each of his questions. Truth typically involves two key components: correspondence and coherence.

Another crucial test in determining truth is Practical tests : whether your beliefs or assertions are practical and applicable to everyday life. This practical test examines a worldview's workability and its practical value in addressing the most significant areas of life and human experience.

Certainly, here's a breakdown of how each worldview element or discipline matches with the correct questions:

Ultimate Reality (Metaphysics)-Question: What is the fundamental nature of reality? Is there an ultimate source or essence underlying everything?

God (Theology)-Question: Does a divine being or higher power exist? What are the attributes and nature of this entity?

Nature of the Universe (Cosmology)-Question: How did the universe come into being? What are its fundamental laws and principles?

Human Nature (Anthropology)-Question: What does it mean to be human? What are the characteristics, abilities, and limitations of human beings?

Knowledge (Epistemology)-Question: How do we acquire knowledge? What are the sources, methods, and limits of human understanding?

Ethics-Question: What is the basis for moral values and principles? How should individuals and societies determine right and wrong actions?

Purpose-Question: What is the purpose or meaning of life? Is there a larger, overarching goal or objective that guides human existence?

These questions correspond to the respective worldview elements or disciplines and are essential for understanding and evaluating different philosophical and belief systems.

Here are few steps for testing a worldview:

- **Earnest Seeking for Truth**: This involves genuinely and actively seeking truth, being open to different perspectives, and striving for a deeper understanding of reality.
- **Coherence and Correspondence Testing**:
  Correspondence Test: This test involves checking if statements or claims align with reality. For instance, if someone says a car parked outside is red, you can go out and verify the color to confirm correspondence to truth.

  Coherence Test: This test assesses the internal consistency and logic of a worldview. In a courtroom scenario, for example, if someone claims they didn't commit a murder, the judge can analyze all their statements to see if they fit together logically and form a coherent narrative.

- Testing for Coherence, Correspondence, and Practicality:

Logical consistency: Answers must be logically consistent or are there obvious contradictions. The aim of logic is the elaboration of a coherent system that allows us to investigate, classify, and evaluate good and bad forms of reasoning.

Warrantability is another critical aspect, representing the justification or evidence supporting a suggestion or claim. Various forms of warrantability include:

Semantic Warrantability: The meaning and usage of terms and concepts are clear and consistent within a given context.

Logical Warrantability: Arguments and reasoning follow logical principles and are free from fallacies.

Systemic Warrantability: The overall structure and organization of a worldview or argument are well-defined and coherent.

Empirical Warrantability: Claims are supported by empirical evidence, observations, or data from the physical world.

Testimonial Warrantability: Justification is based on credible testimony or authoritative sources.

Logical warrantability specifically relies on principles such as the Laws of Identity (entities are what they are), Non-Contradiction (a statement cannot be both true and false at the same time in the same context), and the Excluded Middle (a statement is either true or false, with no middle ground). These logical laws form the foundation for assessing the logical coherence and validity of arguments and beliefs within a worldview or system of thought.

Empirical adequacy: Refers to the ability to verify truth claims through empirical evidence, such as observations, documentation, sources, and data, rather than solely relying on religious texts or faith-based beliefs. This can be particularly relevant when assessing claims related to events like resurrection from death, archaeological findings, or the historical accuracy of a worldview. Here are examples of sources or evidence that can support such claims:

Archaeological Evidence: Physical artifacts, ruins, inscriptions, and structures discovered through archaeological excavations can provide tangible evidence supporting historical events or claims.

Historical Records: Documents, manuscripts, and historical accounts from reliable and unbiased sources can corroborate events or details mentioned in religious texts or traditional narratives.

Scientific Research: Scientific studies, experiments, and analyses can provide empirical data and explanations for phenomena that may be associated with a worldview, such as natural events or processes.

Eyewitness Testimony: Firsthand accounts from credible eyewitnesses or contemporary witnesses can offer valuable testimony supporting specific events or occurrences.

Cross-Cultural Corroboration: When similar events or narratives are found across different cultures, regions, or historical periods, it can strengthen the credibility of those claims.

Forensic Evidence: Forensic analysis, including DNA testing, carbon dating, and other forensic techniques, can provide scientific evidence relevant to historical or archaeological claims.

Secondary Sources: Academic studies, peer-reviewed articles, and scholarly research can provide critical analysis and interpretations of historical or empirical data, offering additional insights and perspectives.

Overall, empirical adequacy relies on a range of sources and evidence beyond religious texts, emphasizing the importance of objective verification and validation through empirical methods and critical examination.

Experiential relevance: All of this should be relevant to your Life. Atheism may claim, there is no real basis for values or morality and therefore morals don't exist. Its relative they say.. If we kill a baby, is it evil or what? Atheism has no foundation for objective morality, since man is product of Time, Chance and Matter. After all what can a product of mere chemical evolution of carbon-based molecules in a "primordial soup can teach us about right and wrong." Atheism believes what is known as 'God of the Gaps'. The "gaps" points out the fallacy of relying on teleological (Intelligent deliberate design) arguments for God's existence. This argument means, "I can't understand it, therefore God did it." Like for instance, throughout history, various natural phenomena that weren't immediately understood, such as lightning, earthquakes, or diseases, were often attributed to the actions of gods or other supernatural entities. As scientific knowledge expanded and provided natural explanations for these phenomena, the need for supernatural explanations diminished. And of course God disappears as the gaps close. The attributes of God in which they atheists assume are different from the attributes of God a theistic thinker makes. The teleological or physico-theological argument, also known as the argument from design, or intelligent design argument is an argument for the existence of God or, more generally, for an intelligent creator based on perceived evidence of deliberate design in the natural world and the universe. Designed for a purpose. Fine tuning of the whole universe for instance.

Who is God? He is the nonphysical, infinite, timeless, personal, intelligent, moral, valuable, Holy, first cause, who has given us intrinsic worth and whom we can know by personal experience.

He is the only entity in existence, the reason for whose existence is in himself. All other entities or quantities exists by virtue of something else.

Science cannot tell us for instance whether a poem or work of literature or a work of art and music is good or beautiful. And when Isaac Newton for example discovered his law of gravity and wrote down the equations of motion, he did not say "marvellous I now understand it. I have got a mechanism, therefore I do not need God." In fact it was the exact opposite. It was because he understood the complexity of sophistication of the mathematical description of the universe that his praise for God was increased. Here we are confusing between Mechanism vs Agency. We have a mechanism that does XYZ therefore there's no need for an agent. God is the agent for the sophistication of the mechanism, and science rejoices in finding such mechanisms, is evidence for the sheer wonder of the creative genius of God.

John C. Lennox, God's Undertaker: Has Science Buried God? Please find below an extract from his book,

"Science has been spectacularly successful in probing the nature of the physical universe and elucidating the mechanisms by which the universe works. Scientific research has also led to the eradication of many horrific diseases, and raised hopes of eliminating many more. And scientific investigation has had another effect in a completely different direction: it has served to relieve a lot of people from superstitious fears. For instance, people need no longer think that an eclipse of the moon is caused by some frightful demon, which they have to placate. For all of these and myriad other things we should be very grateful. But in some quarters the very success of science has also led to the idea that, because we can understand the mechanisms of the universe without bringing in God, we can safely conclude that there was no God who designed and created the universe in the first place. However, such reasoning involves a common logical fallacy, which we can illustrate as follows.

Take a Ford motor car. It is conceivable that someone from a remote part of the world, who was seeing one for the first time and who knew nothing about modern engineering, might imagine that there is a god (Mr. Ford) inside the engine, making it go. He might further imagine that when the engine ran sweetly it was because Mr. Ford inside the engine liked him, and when it refused to go it was because Mr. Ford did not like him. Of course, if he were subsequently to study engineering and take the engine to pieces, he would discover that there is no Mr.

Ford inside it. Neither would it take much intelligence for him to see that he did not need to introduce Mister Ford as an explanation for its working. His grasp of the impersonal principles of internal combustion would be altogether enough to explain how the engine works. So far, so good. But if he then decided that his understanding of the principles of how the engine works made it impossible to believe in the existence of Mr. Ford who designed the engine in the first place, this would be patently false – in philosophical terminology he would be committing a category mistake. Had there never been a Mr. Ford to design the mechanisms, none would exist for him to understand.

It is likewise a category mistake to suppose that our understanding of the impersonal principles according to which the universe works makes it either unnecessary or impossible to believe in the existence of a personal creator who designed, made, and upholds the universe. In other words, we should not confuse the mechanisms by which the universe works either with its cause or its upholder."

What is Truth?

This is the most important or greatest question that any human being can ask. I started my quest asking this question to myself. I was no more interested in fiction or anything which is unreal. Because those things never give us a meaning to our life. When we ask ourselves this question and travel through life's different paths in search of Truth, we end up in a person called Jesus Christ.

"Truth is that which affirms propositionally the nature of reality as it is." Which means the content remains same no matter whatever way we analyse it. It does not need any Fact to support it.

What is our trouble? Well basically it is this. Our Bible reading takes us into what, for us, is quite a new world - namely, the Near eastern world as it was thousands of years ago, primitive, barbaric, unmechanised, agriculture based. God dealing with Jews, Abraham, Moses and later Jesus. It is all intensely interesting but far away. It all belongs to that world, not to this world currently. We feel that we are so to speak, on the outside of Bible. While it is clear that God accomplished so much in those times, how can we capture and apply those divine acts in a way that is relevant for our digital age. We believe there is a large gap or chasm between the truths of the two worlds. We cannot see how it links…… The link is GOD Himself.

There is an ancient proverb, "What is true is not new and what is new is not true." It is a good rule after reading a new book never allow yourself another new one till you have read an old one in between. Every age has its own outlook. There is this subject called "Chronological snobbery". It is defined as the uncritical acceptance of the intellectual climate of our own age and the assumption that whatever has gone out of date is on that count discredited. In other words, we take for granted that the prevailing ideas of our time and culture are unquestionably true. Whatever in the past has been inferior and untrue.

Jesus said, *"every teacher of the law who has been instructed about the kingdom of Heaven is like the owner of a house who brings out of his storeroom new treasures as well as old."* (Matthew 13:52,NIV).

Generations have questioned this sense of remoteness from the biblical experience of God. This is the same question or remoteness we face, when our young son tells us, *"Dad or Mom… Chill, you don't know how to do this or you are not equipped for this or you do not relate or belong………….."* Your son's snobbish remark does not annihilate the fact that, what we see, understand and interpret is unreal. People of each generation have their own character, worldly wisdom, worldly truth, purposes, life and their own generation of sons and daughters…

God encounters with similar questions across all ages, as people in each era inquire based on their prevailing beliefs, wisdom, truth, and thoughts of the time. God's unwavering response to a generation around 700-600 BC, as conveyed through Isaiah, serves as a reminder of their origins and early days.

Isaiah 40: 21-26,NIV, *"Do you not know? Have you not heard? Has it not been told you from the beginning? Have you not understood since the earth was founded? He sits enthroned above the circle of the earth, and its people are like **grasshoppers**. He stretches out the heavens like a canopy, and spreads them out like a tent to live in. He brings princes to naught and reduces the rulers of this world to nothing. No sooner are they planted, no sooner are they sown, no sooner do they take root in the ground, than he blows on them and they wither, and a whirlwind sweeps them away like chaff.*

*"To whom will you compare Me? Or who is My equal?" says the Holy One. Lift up your eyes and look to the heavens: Who **created** all these? He who brings out the starry host one by one and calls forth each of them by name. Because of His great power and mighty strength, not one of them is missing."*

Does not this scripture portion allude to the reality we experience in life? The lifespan of a grasshopper is approximately one year. It does not sit or walk steadily, it keeps changing and jumps around. People of each generation have their own specific character, own worldly wisdom, own worldly truth, own purposes, own life, own sons and daughters… Each of these aspects change or are mutable. But God does not change !!

Do we know, why men worship God….? The short answer is, man changes, but **God does not change**. God does not change His character, His truth, His wisdom, His purpose, His life and His own Son. They are Immutable. So we can trust Him.

God inhabits in eternity says Isaiah, He is not affected by change in time. Isaiah 57:15, *"For thus says the One Who is high and lifted up, **Who inhabits eternity**, Whose name is Holy."*

We worship Him, because He does not change as we do. But unfortunately we do not understand this, in this time bound age, because there is nothing in this world to compare with this immutable character of God. There is no reference point for us to hang on to, God is incomprehensible. He is not comparable as stated in Isaiah 40 portion. We men try our best to address everything with a basic yardstick or reference level with everything in life.. evaluating and comparing. The history of <u>artificial intelligence (AI)</u> dates back to antiquity – intelligent robots appear in the myths of many ancient societies, including Greek, Arabic, Egyptian and Chinese. AI is also something which is being compared to Human Intelligence. But God is not something which cannot be compared with anything we know. AI has also evolved or originated from a human intelligence. We always need to know the origin of a concept, theory, intelligence, product, process or anything in order to invent or discover something new in this world. God does not have an Origin. He is the Origin. He was always there. God Himself is the first and last. Jesus in Matthew 24:35, *"Heaven and earth will pass away, but My words will not pass away."* The word of God will never pass away! It means everything you see in your physical changes and vanishes but not God and the Word which has come from His mouth.

The two unchangeable things are God's character and the word which comes from His mouth. A computer or machine achieves its task or objective when it maintains consistency and immutability in its features and commands. However, these machines falter when their necessary features do not meet requirements or when commands deviate. These nuances are best comprehended by computer technicians or mechanics. God's unchangeable character and His word can only be perceived vividly by a child of God or an heir of promise. Infact God desires to show Himself this to His heirs of promise. If we cannot perceive God, lets first of all approach Him as his beloved children. Jesus taught that one can access the Kingdom of God only by being like a child. The below passage reflects and confirms it.

Hebrews 6:13-18, *"For when God made a promise to Abraham, since He had no one greater by whom to swear, He swore by Himself, saying, "Surely I will bless you and multiply you." And thus Abraham, having patiently waited, obtained the promise. For people swear by something greater than themselves, and in all their disputes an oath is final for confirmation. So when God desired to show more convincingly to the heirs of the promise the **unchangeable character of His purpose, He guaranteed it with an oath**, so that by two unchangeable things, in which it is impossible for God to lie, we who have fled for refuge might have strong encouragement to hold fast to the hope set before us."*

Above all, Bible is the word that speaks unchangeable truth into your life. Unless you read it, you will not understand what I am saying. This is the truth that can drive your life to its fullness. At a point in life, when everything else fails and we reach a point of despair, the only thing we can grip on to, is an eternal truth. Bible guides us, with a wisdom-driven life rather than a situation-driven life.

Consider the implications of having more than one wife. It leads to the loss of unity, as love cannot be equally shared among them by a single husband. This rings true, doesn't it? God has not provided multiple paths to the truth of eternal life; there is only one option — Jesus Christ. He declared, "I am the truth," leaving no other way that God has given. Partial truths are found in other beliefs, I would not disagree with that, but the fullness of truth came through Jesus Christ. No man in history has ever quoted that - 'I am the truth, the way and the life.'

Pilate famously asked Jesus, "What is Truth?" but then walked away without realizing he was turning his back on the most significant question and the ultimate authority of Truth.

An anecdote illustrates this: A man touring Paris with a host visited the Music Hall and Arts but expressed dislike. The Host's response was profound: "They aren't on trial, you are." Similarly, Pilate and the Jewish leaders thought they were judging Christ, but they were, infact, being judged by the Truth itself. This demonstrates the power and nature of Truth—it reaches a point where the Bible seems to read you. The word of God says, when you understand the truth, the truth can set you free. This is not just a quote. Every true Christ follower experiences it.

1Timothy 3:16-17,NIV, discusses the mystery of godliness: *"Beyond all question, the mystery from which true godliness springs is great: He appeared in the flesh, was vindicated by the Spirit, was seen by angels, was preached among the nations, was believed on in the world, was taken up in glory. Now to the King eternal, immortal, invisible, the only God, be honor and glory forever and ever. Amen."*

This passage highlights the mystery and greatness of true godliness and emphasizes the centrality of Christ in the message of salvation. It underscores the authority of God's Word and the importance of preaching the gospel to all nations.

Psalm 119:160 states, *"The sum of Your word is truth, and every one of Your righteous rules endures forever."* This means that truth encompasses the entirety of wisdom, knowledge, and understanding found in the Bible. Truth is like a beautiful pearl necklace, where each pearl is a valuable piece. The beauty of truth becomes apparent and comprehensible when all the pearls are strung together on a single thread... This reality of Truth becomes evident like a well-connected chain of pearl necklace of events as you read from Genesis to Revelation. It is like uncovering a grand design, where every piece fits together to form a complete picture.

Matthew 22:16, *"Teacher, we know that you are true and teach the way of God truthfully, and you do not care about anyone's opinion, for you are not swayed by appearances.*

JESUS said Truth is something which comes from the Father, John17:8. We can travel with God, only if we live in truth. There is also a need to speak truth to each other. But unfortunately this is on a decline.

What truth do we keep in our hearts? What truth do we speak to each other? Do we use truth to communicate with each other? Jesus consistently emphasized that He spoke only what was revealed to Him by the Father in Heaven, without expressing anything of His own accord.

During the 40 days in the desert, Satan presented truth in a way that portrayed bread as a fundamental human need. However, Jesus demonstrated that the Word of God is our essential human requirement. This illustrates how we can be deceived by the world's version of truth. Satan's version of truth aims to bring suffering to God's children. Conversely, God prioritizes the spiritual realm, to seek the kingdom of God, knowing that everything else will follow suit. For example, when the four men lowered the paralytic through the roof, Jesus initially addressed the paralytic' spiritual need by saying, "Your sins are forgiven," before addressing his physical healing.

The truth of the world always prioritizes your physical need above everything else, which is a deception. While God promises to meet all our physical needs, prioritizing the pursuit of His kingdom and truth comes first.

We are familiar with Stalin, the Russian dictator responsible for the extermination of 15 million of his own country's people. His life story began as a seminary student, yet he became a man guided by falsified truths. Malcolm Mugridge, a renowned journalist, interviewed Stalin's daughter, Svetlana, about her father.

She quotes, Stalin was questioned once about how he could cause such suffering to people. Stalin called for a live chicken. Forcefully clutching the chicken in one hand, with the other he began to systematically pluck out its feathers. As the chicken struggled in vain to escape, he continued with the painful denuding until the bird was completely stripped. "Now you watch," Stalin said as he placed the chicken on the floor and walked away with some breadcrumbs in his hand. Incredibly, the fear-crazed chicken hobbled toward him and clung to the legs of his trousers. Stalin threw a handful of grain to the bird, and it began to follow him around the room, he turned to his dumbfounded colleagues and said quietly, "This is the way to rule the people. Did you see how that chicken followed me for food, even though I had caused it such torture? People are like that chicken. If you inflict inordinate pain on them, they will follow you for food the rest of their lives."

What can a false Truth do to the conscience of a man like Stalin, ex-seminary student. It is often said that Satan is the father of lies and deception, and one of his strategies is to distort or present a twisted version of the truth to inflict harm and confusion. This can manifest in various ways, such as manipulating facts, distorting perceptions, or promoting false ideologies that lead people away from God's truth and into darkness or harm. It is a reminder to be discerning and rely on God's wisdom and guidance to recognize and resist falsehoods. Stalin punched his fist toward God as he died of sickness. The world witnessed a bloodbath of millions under the disguise of a falsified Truth. God's Truth sets us free in spirit, soul and body. Truth is a very key factor of our being. When encountering various truths, it is essential for each of us to reflect on whether they genuinely resonate with our human experiences and circumstances. Those rigorous themes and worldviews get rather tiresome. After some time, you are sort of beating the same horse again and again. Answering the same question or granted it may be a fresh question for a questioner. We must exercise caution when solely relying on rigid logical arguments for truth, as an overemphasis on intellectual reasoning, it can detach all your faith, all your faith becomes cerebral. When you wrestle with intensely philosophical issues, there is a great danger of getting so slanted that the bridge between the head and the heart never ever gets connected and it is critical that amputation – does not take place. There has to be a connection between the head and the heart. Jesus Himself gave His message in parables, in a way that mystified His listeners because He did not want to always lay it on the lowest shelf. He said, you need to seek, need to pursue and then you will find. They will search for me and find me, and when you search for me with all your heart, soul and mind - there is that pursuit element which is very critical for our search of truth.

Indeed, acknowledging the **corruption within our own hearts is a profound truth** which we need to accept in the first place. The concept of inherent sin, often referred to as original sin, acknowledges that humans are born with a tendency or inclination towards sin due to the Fall in the Garden of Eden. This inherent sin condition affects the entire world, leading to corruption and separation from God. Understanding this reality helps us grasp the need for redemption and the significance of Christ's sacrificial work in restoring our relationship with God. Yes, according to the biblical narrative, the presence of God's glory and the fullness of the Holy Spirit were affected by the introduction of sin into the world through Adam and Eve. The story of the Fall in Genesis describes how humanity's disobedience led to a separation from God's immediate presence and the loss of the perfect relationship that existed prior to sin. This separation highlighted the need for reconciliation and restoration.

The Christian faith is the only faith that claims a supernatural new birth. No one else claims this. No worldview claims this. The new birth is being born out of the Holy Spirit. But for this, we need to have faith, humility and understanding about the Spirit, God started with the Hebrews, the blueprint of true Godliness was revealed to them, in various dispensations of time. God chose a single man, Abraham, before choosing a nation. He decided to bless the whole world through this man of faith. No favours or partiality. It was His choice… God made numerous promises to Abraham, including that his descendants (seeds) would be as countless as the sands of the sea and the stars in the sky. Additionally, God promised that the entire world would be blessed through Abraham.

Jesus came as a descendant of Abraham after approximately 42 generations, depending on how one counts generations in the genealogies presented in the Bible. The fullness of blessing for all humanity was realized through Christ Jesus who was the seed or offspring of Abraham. Christ's arrival marked the restoration of God's Spirit into the sinful world, granting everyone access to the Holy Spirit through faith in Him. This event is known as the New Covenant or the New Testament. In contrast, before this, God's Spirit was only anointed upon specific individuals and provided exclusively to certain people in the Old Testament or Old Covenant. Absolutely, in the New Covenant through Christ, the scope of God's blessings and access to His Spirit expanded to include the entire world. It became an inclusive covenant, offering salvation and the indwelling of the Holy Spirit to all who believe in Jesus Christ, regardless of their background or status.

The Bible says He chose the nation of Israel, though they were the weakest and smallest in the whole world in the Old Covenant. Abraham was seen as the father of their nation. Abraham is considered the Father of believers among three leading faiths. But the promise to Abraham was not just earthly blessings, it was the promise of the Holy Spirit to the whole world. God in us !! **This is the truth, which is still unveiled to many**. This is the most delicate domain where the truth remains unacknowledged. Abraham's own son Issac was spared from a sacrifice by God at Mount Moriah, instead, God said to Abraham, " Jehovah Jireh" (God will provide, Me Myself, I will provide). Yes, in the story of Abraham and Isaac, God provided a ram as a substitute for Isaac, sparing him from being sacrificed. This event highlights God's provision and mercy, showing that He always provides the perfect sacrifice. It is a foreshadowing of the ultimate sacrifice of Jesus Christ, the spotless Lamb of God, who would later fulfill the requirement for atonement for sin once and for all. Up to this point, all three prominent faiths acknowledge and align with this scripture. Their differences lie in their interpretations of what God promised as a substitute for Abraham's son, whom He said, **He would provide.**

Three attributes of God are His **Justice, His Love and His Righteousness**. God applies these attributes, in all His decisions and actions, unlike us humans. We struggle to consistently activate all three attributes at the same time. But God does it all the time.

Jeremiah 9:24, *"But let him who boasts boast in this, that he understands and knows Me, that I am the Lord who practices **steadfast love, justice, and righteousness** in the earth. For in these things I delight, declares the Lord."*

The Mount called Calvary became the convergence point in human history, where God provided His own Son as a sacrifice, where the Truth of God's steadfast love, rightful justice and righteousness met together to release the fullness of the promise to Abraham to all mankind. By conquering sin, fulfilling God's law, accomplishing justice, paying the debt, achieving victory over death, and demonstrating redemption through His love, Jesus Christ displayed His sacrifice to the entire world on the Cross as the spotless Lamb.

The Bible says that the Lamb was slain before the foundation of the world. This means God's entry into mankind was a sovereign redemption plan even before the creation of the world. Jesus Christ, the Son of God, was the lamb that God promised Abraham that He would provide. Jesus Christ was the promised seed of Abraham. The book of Romans and Galatians provides in-depth wisdom about this subject.

"*So that in Christ Jesus the blessing of Abraham might come to the <u>nations</u>, so that we might receive the promised Spirit through faith.*" (Galatians 3: 14).

Charles Sobhraj, was a notorious prisoner who escaped jail several times, only to be captured again on each of his attempts to be free. During his jailbreaks, he believed he was free, but in reality, he was not truly free. If the court had granted him forgiveness, then he would have genuinely experienced freedom. He would have become FREE INDEED.

Being free and Being Free indeed are two different things. John 8:36, "*If the Son sets you free, you will be free indeed.*" Freedom from sin and receive God's salvation.

Through our experience and reality, the world's truth grants us temporary freedom, yet leading to the following outcome:

1. Ends in shame like the Sobhraj story.
2. No eternal inheritance or possessions.
3. No protection or seal.
4. No Guarantee.

God's Truth in Christ :

1. Covers, seals and protects eternally.
2. There is a valid guarantee eternally.
3. Inheritance and possessions eternally.
4. Ends in Glory.

Ephesians1:13-14, "*<u>In Him</u> you also, when you heard the <u>**word of truth**</u>, the gospel of your salvation, and believed in Him, were <u>**sealed with the promised** Holy Spirit</u>, Who is the <u>**guarantee** of our **inheritance**</u> until we acquire possession of it, to the praise of His <u>**glory**</u>.*"

TRUE FREEDOM IS ETERNAL GLORY THROUGH CHRIST JESUS WHO IS THE GUARANTEE, THE SEAL, THE FORERUNNER IN OUR INHERITANCE.

"For the law was given through Moses; grace and truth came through Jesus Christ." (John1:17).

Chapter 5

Logical Consequences of Atheism

Let us consider a dialogue between a Defender of Theism and an Atheist.

Defender: When it comes to the logical consequences of atheism, remember there is no free will, we are just complex biochemical reactions. How do we change behaviour - is it by changing the environment and by injecting chemicals or giving a person drugs? I abhor that, I call that brainwashing. Yes, I insist that human beings are created in the image of God, have a free will and therefore the way that I change you, is not by giving you drugs or just changing your environment. I seek to reason with you, I appeal to your conscience. I appeal to your emotions, I appeal to your experience and I say, 'Come on friend wake up and smell the coffee.' You know very well that slavery and racism are not just subjectively wrong, you know it is objectively absolutely wrong, and that is the way you choose to live your life. But you have a contradiction with your philosophical position of atheism because if you are going to be consistent with your atheism or agnosticism, it does not allow for an objective morality. See the only way you can have an objective moral, is if there is more to reality than matter and energy. There is got to be a moral lawgiver with a thinking mind, who says human life is valuable for a reason. And if you mess with human life and destroy human life, that is really evil; and it is really good, if you build up human life, yeah because life is a wonderful thing.

Response: Yeah, I agree, but um… if there is moral lawgiver, life is a wonderful thing !! We're all trying to figure that out….

D: You better try and figure it out. I hope you come to a conclusion pretty soon, it is a rather important question.

R: Why is human life valuable, can you tell me?

D: Yeah, I sure can, because he, she and you are all created by God for a purpose, and you are created to love God with your heart, soul, mind and strength and to love your neighbour as yourself. Which means all of you guys have innate value. You do not have value, just because you are a nice guy. And I guess, if I tell you all that, you are just wonderful guys, you all have value, aren't I also wonderful, - No! That is not how you possess value !! What I want to convey, is that it is just a subjective arbitrary personal opinion of mine. In reality, these guys have innate value, because they are not cosmic accidents, they are human beings created in the image of God, for a purpose. That is why they have got value. You take God out of the picture, you are up a creek without a paddle, when it comes to explaining why these guys have value.

R: What if you take us out of the picture? Where's god?

D: And sir I hate to tell you, if you and I did not exist, all these people around here would still exist, right? The existence of these people does not depend on you and me.

R: If the world ends tomorrow, if life itself is consciousness, that perceiving all of this around us is gone, is there anything here?

D: Yeah, if there are no human beings alive tomorrow, the tree is still going to be there.

R: No, I am saying, all life, all life is gone, yes all. Life is gone, is there still god?

D: Yeah, and God is a living being.

R: How do you perceive it?

D: Yeah, perception does not define reality. I do not agree with the line of thinking, that says perception defines reality. That is bogus, my perception can be wrong. Part of, why I like education is, I have got to learn to get my perceptions in line with reality. That is called being an educated person. Understanding what is real, I am convinced God is real. I am convinced Jesus Christ is real, that is why faith in Him, is so wise. Because that is getting in touch with reality ..

R: My question still remains, Where is God without us? Still living?

D: Just fine, He does not need me or you.

R: Where is He living in heaven? Where's heaven? Another dimension?

D: Yes, God is in another dimension, God is not limited to space and time, He is outside of space and time.

R: You know about this dimension better than I do. I have never been in another dimension, How can you say there is a god? How can I say there is a god, if we do not know anything about the dimension?

D: Because it is real clear for me, from the order and design in this universe, that there is got to be a designer. It is clear that this universe has a beginning. If this universe has a beginning, it has got to have a cause. There has got to be an uncaused cause otherwise there would be an infinite regress, which is illogical. So, therefore, the best explanation of an uncaused cause, who caused the universe, is a thinking mind, an intelligent designer.., that is where you start in your understanding of who God is.

R: Where did the intelligent designer come from?

D: He is Eternal. Intelligent eternally, no beginning, therefore He does not need to have a cause. See, if you do not have a beginning, you do not have to have a cause. But if you have a beginning, you got to have a cause. Something, just does not happen by chance. There is a cause. You and I walking through the woods, we see a ball, you say hey man-how'd the ball get here? I say it did not get here, it just is, that does not make sense, the ball was put there by somebody. Go from the ball in the woods to the earth, hey man-how'd it get here? It did not get here, it just is. That is absurdity !! No, someone caused it, to be here.

R: And who's caused that someone? What and when at a certain point…it's 'just is'? There has to be 'just is'.There's this Is-ness.

D: Well, the way I would put it - at some point you are going to have to face the fact, that there is an eternal someone and that eternal is God. That is this God.. There is an eternal uncaused cause that caused the universe to come into being, which is GOD.

How do we live in a society with total secularized consciousness?

Steve Turner, an English journalist describes secularism as follows,

We believe in Marx, Freud and Darwin.
We believe everything is OK
as long as you don't hurt anyone,
to the best of your definition of hurt,
and to the best of your knowledge.

We believe in sex before, during and after marriage.
We believe in the therapy of sin.
We believe that adultery is fun.
We believe that taboos are taboo.

We believe that everything's getting better,
despite evidence to the contrary.
The evidence must be investigated.
You can prove anything with evidence.

We believe there's something in horoscopes,
UFO's and bent spoons;
Jesus was a good man just like Buddha
Mohammed and ourselves.
He was a good moral teacher although we
think his good morals were bad.

We believe that all religions are basically the same,
at least the one that we read was.
They all believe in love and goodness.
They only differ on matters of
creation, sin, heaven, hell, God and salvation.

We believe that after death comes The Nothing
because when you ask the dead what happens
they say Nothing.
If death is not the end, if the dead have lied,
then it's compulsory heaven for all
excepting perhaps Hitler, Stalin and Genghis Khan.

We believe in Masters and Johnson.
What's selected is average.
What's average is normal.
What's normal is good.

We believe in total disarmament.
We believe there are direct links between
warfare and bloodshed.

Americans should beat their guns into
tractors and the Russians would be sure to follow.

We believe that man is essentially good.
It's only his behaviour that lets him down.
This is the fault of society.
Society is the fault of conditions.
Conditions are the fault of society.

We believe that each man must find the truth
that is right for him.
Reality will adapt accordingly.
The universe will readjust. History will alter.
We believe that there is no absolute truth
excepting the truth that there is no absolute truth.

We believe in the rejection of creeds & flowering of individual thought.
Then he puts this Postscript:
If chance be
the Father of all flesh,
disaster is his rainbow in the sky
and when you hear:

State of Emergency!
Sniper Kills Ten!
Troops on Rampage!
Whites go Looting!
Bomb blasts school !

It is but the sound of man
worshipping his maker.

We are redefining reality, we are reconstituting the actual truth of things. We are perverting our thoughts. We play word games, deceitful in the usage of truth. It is important that we find our definitions, find our coherence and cogency in the legitimate representation of what is essentially true. All definitions have been destroyed of human essence, purpose, meaning and essential worth.!! Poets are more truthful.

Chapter 6

Designer God - Uncaused First Cause

Order and design points to a Designer with a mind. When we see a creative painting or a design, we know that it was created by a thinking personality.

Question: I understand that you argue, a painting or a creation implies a creator, as a painting suggests a painter and a design suggests a designer. However, I must ask: if God is timeless, faceless, and immaterial, existing eternally without being caused, who designed God? Why can't nature exist in the same way—eternal, uncaused, faceless, and timeless—just as you describe God? Why can't our uncaused origins be as marvelous and precise as God, but instead be attributed to natural causes?

Answer: Excellent question. You are right that we have two options here, either the universe is the uncaused first cause or something beyond the universe is the uncaused first cause. The problem is that all the evidence points to the fact that the universe is not the uncaused first cause. Let me give you a brief.

- The second law of Thermodynamics - the Law of Entropy, says that the universe is running down. Natural processes tend to move towards a state of greater disorder or randomness. Well, if it is running down, somebody must have wound it up. We would have no energy left right now if the universe was eternal.
- The universe is expanding. Yes, Edwin Hubble's observations in 1929 led to the formulation of Hubble's Law, which showed that the universe is expanding. This discovery provided evidence for the Big Bang Theory, which posits that the universe began from an extremely hot and dense state. This initial state is often referred to as a singularity—a point of infinite density and zero volume. The singularity itself represents a condition where the known laws of physics break down, and it is often described as "nothing" because it precedes the existence

46

of time and space as we understand them. Thus, the expansion of the universe suggests that it had a beginning, emerging from this singularity.

- Radiation Afterglow is known as the Cosmic Microwave Background (CMB) radiation. Discovered by Arno Penzias and Robert Wilson in 1965, the CMB is the remnant heat left over from the Big Bang. This faint glow of radiation permeates the entire universe and provides strong evidence supporting the Big Bang Theory. The existence of the CMB is often described as the "smoking gun" because it directly corroborates the idea that the universe had a hot, dense beginning and has been expanding and cooling ever since.

- The Cosmic Microwave Background (CMB) radiation contains small temperature fluctuations or "seeds" that are crucial for the formation of galaxies. These temperature variations are on the order of just a few parts in 100,000 but represent slight density differences in the early universe. Over time, these density variations grew under the influence of gravity, leading to the formation of gas clouds, stars, and eventually galaxies. Thus, the "galaxy seeds" observed in the CMB helped to shape the large-scale structure of the universe as we see it today.

- Einstein's theory of General Relativity, shows that time, space and matter are co-relative, that they came into existence together. That space, time and matter literally had a beginning. Einstein knew this in 1916, then observational evidence began in 1919 when Eddington did his test on the eclipse. And then Hubble discovered the expanding Universe in 1929 with the radiation afterglow in the great Galaxy seeds. So the evidence points to the fact that the universe is not the uncaused first cause, there must be something beyond the universe. And that thing, that is beyond the universe must be spaceless, timeless and immaterial. And If You're Timeless, would you have a beginning?

Q: No

A: No, so then, God did not have a beginning. He is the uncaused, first cause. Aristotle, Plato, they all knew this, they knew there had to be an unmoved mover from another dimension.

Q: But then why is there theology, why do we worship God?

A: Excellent point you don't have to worship God. In fact, Aristotle never worshipped God. Greeks never got their theology and philosophy together. They knew that there had to be an unmoved mover, but they never put the two together and worshipped the unmoved Mover.

Q: On that point do you have the free will to accept or reject God, but the obvious conclusion is that the rejection of God will lead to Eternal damnation and death. So, in reality we do not really have the choice to accept or not to accept God. You must ultimately accept God, assuming we choose to avoid perdition. You don't Have To Worship the unmoved Mover; you don't have to. You can do whatever you want, that's why you have free will. God loves you enough to give you free will. You can love Him or reject Him, that's up to you.

A: But let me back up for a second. There are only two possibilities. If God exists, in eternity you're going to be with him or you're not going to be with him, Right? That's logically the only two options. If you want to be with him, you will seek him out and be with him. If you don't want to be with him, God will not force you into His presence against your will.

In fact, let me make the objection stronger than what you're making it.

During a debate at the University of Michigan, Eddie Tabash, an atheist attorney from Beverly Hills, posed a challenging question about his mother, a Holocaust survivor who had rejected the gospel: Was she in hell? The speaker responded, acknowledging uncertainty about her final moments but stating that if she didn't accept faith, God wouldn't force her into His presence against her will, as God is too loving for that.

The speaker then engaged the audience with a hypothetical scenario about unwanted romantic pursuit, asking if any women had been pursued by someone they didn't want to date. He humorously noted that some might feel this way about the person sitting next to them. He explained that if a man continues to pursue a woman despite her rejection and declares he will force her to love him, it's impossible because love must be freely given.

True love would mean leaving her alone, which the speaker likened to God's approach. God continuously reaches out to people, but if they persistently reject Him, He eventually gives them up to their own desires. This, the speaker explained, is what hell represents—separation from God and a place where one can continue to reject Him but is confined. Hell is described as a quarantine of evil, while Heaven is being in God's presence. God loves people too much to force them into His presence against their will.

If there exists an uncaused first cause of the universe, an unmoved mover, does that automatically mean that this entity deserves our worship? This question delves into a deeper understanding of who God is beyond mere scientific reasoning. The discussions about God as the creative force behind the universe or the intelligent designer are just the starting point. It is like stepping onto a stone to progress further along the path of understanding.

Once we grasp the logical necessity of an uncaused first cause, and recognize that the universe itself cannot create matter, we start to contemplate the concept of God as the creator. However, this is just the beginning of a cumulative case for Christianity that becomes increasingly compelling as it unfolds.

The journey leads to something deeply personal. In the New Testament, Jesus explained why He used parables as a means of communication — to convey truths to those who are receptive while concealing them from those who are resistant.

It is about having ears to hear and eyes to see, about being open to truth wherever it leads. When we take a step toward the possibility of God, He reciprocates by drawing near to us.

My challenge to those reading this is not to confine oneself to the limitations of science as the sole means of knowing truth. Personal experiences, relationships, and spiritual connections go beyond what can be dissected under a microscope. Just as I know my wife's love for me through deeper levels of understanding, I know God through a relationship with Him. He walks with me, speaks to me, and reveals Himself in ways that are deeply personal and transformative.

The essence of Christianity lies in the Incarnation — God presenting Himself to us in a way that we can know Him. Jesus Christ, as Immanuel, God With Us, embodies the image of the invisible God. To understand God's character, motives, and mission, we look to Jesus' life, ministry, death, resurrection, and ascension.

In conclusion, conversations about God should not remain confined to theoretical or abstract realms. They should be personal, relational, and deeply meaningful.

Chapter 7
Big Bang- Beginning

Einstein did not believe it was possible.

Stephen Hawking said it might be the greatest scientific discovery of all time.

What discovery has baffled the greatest scientific minds of the past century, and why has it caused them to rethink the origin of our universe? New, more powerful, telescopes have revealed mysteries about our universe that have raised new questions about the origin of life. Oxygen under Pacific ocean. Until now, scientists thought oxygen was only made using energy from sunlight. The discovery of "dark oxygen" being made at more than 13,000 feet below the ocean's surface challenges that theory. I think we therefore need to revisit questions like: where could aerobic life have begun?.

Has science discovered God?

But wait a minute! Has not science proven we do not need God to explain the universe? Lightning, earthquakes and even babies used to be explained as acts of God. But now we know better. What is it about this discovery that is so fundamentally different, and why has it stunned the scientific world?

This discovery and what molecular biologists have learned about the sophisticated coding within DNA have many scientists now admitting that the universe appears to be part of a grand design.

One cosmologist put it this way: "Many scientists, when they admit their views, incline toward the teleological or design argument."

Surprisingly, many scientists who are talking about God have no religious belief whatsoever. So, what are these stunning discoveries that have scientists suddenly speaking of God? Three revolutionary discoveries from the fields of astronomy and molecular biology stand out:

'The universe had a beginning.
The universe is just right for life.
DNA coding reveals intelligence.'

The statements, leading scientists have made about these discoveries may shock you. Let us take a look.

One -Time Beginning

Since the dawn of civilization man has gazed in awe at the stars, wondering what they are and how they got there. Although on a clear night the unaided human eye can see about 6,000 stars, Hubble and other powerful telescopes indicate there are trillions of them clustered in over 100 billion galaxies. Our sun is like one grain of sand amidst the world's beaches.

However, prior to the 20th century, the majority of scientists believed our own Milky Way galaxy was the entire universe, and that only about 100 million stars existed.

Most scientists believed that our universe never had a beginning. They believed mass, space and energy had always existed.

But in the early 20th century, astronomer Edwin Hubble discovered the universe is expanding. Rewinding the process mathematically, he calculated that everything in the universe, including matter, energy, space and even time itself, actually had a beginning.

Shockwaves rang loudly throughout the scientific community.

Many scientists, including Einstein, reacted negatively. In what Einstein later called "the biggest blunder of my life," he fudged the equations to avoid the implication of a beginning.

Perhaps the most vocal adversary of a beginning to the universe was British astronomer Sir Fred Hoyle, who sarcastically nicknamed the creation event a "Big bang." He stubbornly held to his steady state theory that the universe has always existed. So did Einstein and other scientists until the evidence for a beginning became overwhelming. The "elephant in the room" implication of a beginning is that something or Someone beyond scientific investigation must have started it all.

Finally, in 1992, COBE satellite experiments proved that the universe really did have a one-time beginning in an incredible flash of light and energy. Although some scientists called it the moment of creation, most preferred referring to it as the "Big bang."

Astronomer Robert Jastrow tries to help us imagine how it all began. "The picture suggests the explosion of a cosmic hydrogen bomb. The instant in which the cosmic bomb exploded marked the birth of the Universe."

Everything from Nothing

Science is unable to tell us what or who caused the universe to begin. But some believe it clearly points to a Creator. "British theorist, Edward Milne, wrote a mathematical treatise on relativity which concluded by saying, 'As to the first cause of the Universe, in the context of expansion, that is left for the reader to insert, but our picture is incomplete without Him."

Another British scientist, Edmund Whittaker attributed the beginning of our universe to "Divine will constituting Nature from nothingness."

Many scientists were struck by the parallel of a one-time creation event from nothing with the biblical creation account in Genesis 1:1. Prior to this discovery, many scientists regarded the biblical account of creation from nothing as unscientific.

Although he called himself an agnostic, Jastrow was compelled by the evidence to admit, "Now we see how the astronomical evidence leads to a biblical view of the origin of the world."

Another agnostic, George Smoot, the Nobel Prize winning scientist in charge of the COBE experiment, also admits to the parallel. "There is no doubt that a parallel exists between the big bang as an event and the Christian notion of creation from nothing."

Scientists who used to scoff at the Bible as a book of fairy tales, are now admitting that the biblical concept of creation from nothing has been right all along.

Cosmologists, who specialize in the study of the universe and its origins, soon realized that a chance cosmic explosion could never bring about life any more than a nuclear bomb would—unless it was precisely engineered to do so. And that meant a designer must have planned it. They began using words like, "Super-intellect," "Creator," and even "Supreme Being" to describe this designer. Let's look at why.

Finely-Tuned for Life

Physicists calculated that for life to exist, gravity and the other forces of nature needed to be just right or our universe could not exist. Had the expansion rate been slightly weaker, gravity would have pulled all matter back into a "big crunch." We are not talking about merely a one or two percent reduction in the universe's expansion rate.

Stephen Hawking writes, "If the rate of expansion one second after the big bang had been smaller by even one part in a hundred thousand million million, the universe would have re-collapsed before it ever reached its present size."

On the flip side, if the expansion rate had been a mere fraction greater than it was, galaxies, stars and planets could never have formed, and we would not be here.

And for life to exist, the conditions in our solar system and planet also need to be just right. For example, we all realize that without an atmosphere of oxygen, none of us would be able to breathe. And without oxygen, water could not exist. Without water, there would be no rainfall for our crops. Other elements such as hydrogen, nitrogen, sodium, carbon, calcium, and phosphorus are also essential for life.

But that alone is not all that is needed for life to exist. The size, temperature, relative proximity, and chemical makeup of our planet, sun, and moon also need to be just right. And there are dozens of other conditions that needed to be exquisitely fine-tuned or we would not be here to think about it.

Scientists who believe in God may have expected such fine-tuning, but atheists and agnostics were unable to explain the remarkable "coincidences." Theoretical physicist Stephen Hawking, an agnostic, writes, "The remarkable fact is that the values of these numbers seem to have been very finely adjusted to make possible the development of life."

Accident or Miracle?

But couldn't this fine-tuning be attributed to chance? After all, odds-makers know that even long shots can eventually win at the racetrack.

And, against heavy odds, lotteries are eventually won by someone. So, what are the odds against human life existing by chance from a random explosion in cosmic history?

For human life to be possible from a big bang defies the laws of probability. One astronomer calculates the odds at less than 1 chance in a trillion trillion trillion trillion trillion trillion trillion trillion trillion trillion trillion trillion. It would be far easier for a blind-folded person—in one try— to discover one specially marked grain of sand out of all the beaches of the world.

Another example of how unlikely it would be for a random big bang to produce life is one person winning over a thousand consecutive mega- million dollar lotteries after purchasing only a single ticket for each.

What would be your reaction to such news? Impossible—unless it was fixed by someone behind the scenes, which is what everyone would think. And that is what many scientists are concluding—Someone behind the scenes designed and created the universe.

This new understanding of how miraculous human life is in our universe led the agnostic astronomer George Greenstein to ask, "Is it possible that suddenly, without intending to, we have stumbled upon the scientific proof of the existence of a Supreme Being?"

However, as an agnostic, Greenstein maintains his faith in science, rather than a Creator, to ultimately explain our origins.

Jastrow explains why some scientists are reluctant to accept a transcendent Creator, There is a kind of religion in science; it is the religion of a person who believes there is order and harmony in the Universe…This religious faith of the scientist is violated by the discovery that the world had a beginning under conditions in which the known laws of physics are not valid, and as a product of forces or circumstances we cannot discover. When that happens, the scientist has lost control. If he really examined the implications, he would be traumatized.

It is understandable why scientists like Greenstein and Hawking seek other explanations rather than attribute our finely-tuned universe to a Creator. Hawking speculates that other unseen (and unprovable) universes may exist, increasing the odds that one of them (ours) is perfectly fine-tuned for life. However, since his proposal is speculative, and outside of verification, it can hardly be called "scientific." Although he is also an agnostic, British astrophysicist Paul Davies dismisses Hawking's idea as too speculative. He writes, "Such a belief must rest on faith rather than observation."

Although Hawking continues leading the charge to explore purely scientific explanations for our origins, other scientists, including many agnostics, have acknowledged what appears to be overwhelming evidence for a Creator. Hoyle wrote,

"A common sense interpretation of the facts suggests that a superintellect has monkeyed with physics, as well as chemistry and biology, and that there are no blind forces worth speaking about in nature."

Although Einstein was not religious, and did not believe in a personal God, he called the genius behind the universe "an intelligence of such superiority that, compared with it, all the systematic thinking and acting of human beings is an utterly insignificant reflection."

Atheist Christopher Hitchens, who spent much of his life writing and debating against God, was most perplexed by the fact that life could not exist if things were different by just "one degree or one hair."

Davies acknowledges,

There is for me powerful evidence that there is something going on behind it all. It seems as though somebody has fine-tuned nature's numbers to make the Universe…. The impression of design is overwhelming.

Isaiah 40:26, *"Lift up your eyes and look to the heavens: Who created all these? He who brings out the starry host one by one, and calls forth each of them by name. Because of his great power and mighty strength, not one of them is missing."*

Chapter 8

DNA – Language of Life

DNA:The Language of Life

Astronomy is not the only area where science has seen evidence for design. Molecular biologists have discovered intricately complex design in the microscopic world of DNA. In the past century, scientists learned that a tiny molecule called DNA is the "brains" behind each cell in our bodies as well as every other living thing. Yet the more they discover about DNA, the more amazed they are at the brilliance behind it.

Scientists who believe the material world is all that exists (materialists), like Richard Dawkins, argue DNA evolved by Natural selection without a Creator. Yet even most ardent evolutionists admit that the origin of DNA's intricate complexity is unexplainable.

DNA's intricate complexity caused its co-discoverer, Francis Crick, to believe that it could never have originated on Earth naturally. Crick, an evolutionist who believed life is too complex to have originated on Earth, and must have come from outer space, wrote,

'An honest man, armed with all the knowledge available to us now, could only state that in some sense, the origin of life appears at the moment to almost be a miracle, so many are the conditions which would have had to have been satisfied to get it going.'

The coding behind DNA reveals such intelligence that it staggers the imagination. A mere pinhead of DNA contains information equivalent to a stack of paperback books that would encircle the earth 5,000 times. And DNA operates like a language with its own extremely complex software code. Microsoft founder Bill Gates says that the software of DNA is "far, far more complex than any software we have ever developed."

Dawkins and other materialists believe that all this complexity originated through natural selection. Yet, as Crick remarked, natural selection could never have produced the first molecule. Many scientists believe that the coding within the DNA molecule points to an intelligence far exceeding what could have occurred by natural causes.

In the early 21st century, leading atheist Antony Flew's atheism came to an abrupt end when he studied the intelligence behind DNA. Flew explains what changed his opinion.

'What I think the DNA material has done is to show that intelligence must have been involved in getting these extraordinarily diverse elements together. The enormous complexity by which the results were achieved look to me like the work of intelligence…. It now seems to me that the finding of more than fifty years of DNA research have provided materials for a new and enormously powerful argument to design.'

Although Flew was not a Christian, he admitted that the "software" behind DNA is far too complex to have originated without a "designer." The discovery of the incredible intelligence behind DNA has, in this former leading atheist's words, "provided materials for a new and enormously powerful argument to design."

Fingerprints of a Creator

Are scientists now convinced that a Creator has left his "fingerprints" on the universe?

Although many scientists are still bent on squeezing God out of the universe, most recognize the religious implications of these new discoveries. In his book, The Grand Design, Stephen Hawking, who does not believe in a personal God, attempts to explain why the universe does not need God. Yet when faced with the evidence, even Hawking has also admitted, "There must be religious overtones. But I think most scientists prefer to shy away from the religious side of it."

As an agnostic, Jastrow had no Christian agenda behind his conclusions. However, he freely acknowledges the compelling case for a Creator. Jastrow writes of the shock and despair experienced by scientists who thought they had squeezed God out of their world.

"For the scientist who has lived by his faith in the power of reason, the story ends like a bad dream. He has scaled the mountains of ignorance; he is about to conquer the highest peak; as he pulls himself over the final rock, he is greeted by a band of theologians who have been sitting there for centuries."

A Personal Creator?

If there is a superintelligent Creator, the question arises, what is He like? Is He just some Force like in Star Wars, or is He a personal Being like us? Since we are personal and relational beings, would not the One Who created us also be personal and relational?

Many scientists like Arthur L. Schawlow, Professor of Physics at Stanford University, winner of the Nobel Prize in physics, believe that these new discoveries provide compelling evidence for a personal God. He writes, "It seems to me that when confronted with the marvels of life and the universe, one must ask why and not just how. The only possible answers are religious.... I find a need for God in the universe and in my own life."

If God is personal and since he has given us the ability to communicate, would not we expect him to communicate with us and let us know why we are here?

As we have seen, science is unable to answer questions about God and the purpose for life. However, since the Bible was right about creation from nothing, might it also be trustworthy regarding God, life and purpose?

Two thousand years ago a man set foot on our planet who claimed to have the answer to life. Although His time on earth was brief, His impact changed the world, and is still felt today. His name is Jesus Christ.

The eyewitnesses to Jesus Christ tell us that He continually demonstrated creative power over nature's laws. They tell us He was wise, humble and compassionate. He healed the lame, deaf and blind. He stopped raging storms instantly, created food for the hungry on the spot, turned water into wine at a wedding, and even raised the dead. And they claimed after His brutal execution, He rose from the dead. They also tell us that Jesus Christ is the One who flung the stars into space, fine-tuned our universe and the Creator.

Could He be the one of whom Einstein unknowingly referred to as the "superintelligence" behind the universe? Could Jesus Christ be the one of whom Hoyle unknowingly referred to as having "monkeyed with physics, chemistry and biology?"

Has the mystery of who was behind the big bang and the intelligence of DNA been revealed in the following account from the New Testament?

Now Christ is the visible expression of the invisible God. He existed before creation began, for it was through Him that everything was made, whether spiritual or material, seen or unseen. Through Him, and for Him, also, were created power and dominion, ownership and authority. In fact, every single thing was created through, and for Him….Life from nothing began through Him, and life from the dead began through Him, and He is, therefore, justly called **the LORD of All** ! (Colossians1)

Jesus spoke with authority about God's love for us and the reason He created us. He said He has a plan for our lives, and that plan centers on a relationship with Himself. But for that relationship to be possible, Jesus had to die on the cross for our sins. And it was necessary for Him to rise from the dead so that we too could have life after death.

If Jesus is the Creator, He certainly would have the power over life and death. And those closest to Him claim they saw Him alive after He died and was buried for three days.

Founders of modern science were Robert Hoyle,Keller, Issac Newton were theistic scientists who believed in the intelligent designer..

Chapter 9

Radio Metric Dating

The Primary Faulty Assumption

Radioisotope dating of minerals, rocks, and meteorites is perhaps the most-claimed "incontestable" proof for the alleged old age of the earth and the solar system. The declared absolute ages provided by the radioisotope dating methods provide an aura of certainty to the claimed millions and billions of years for the formation of the earth's rocks. Consequently, the scientific community and the general public around the world appear convinced of the earth's claimed great antiquity.

Radiometric dating is a technique used to determine the age of rocks, fossils, and other geological materials based on the decay of radioactive isotopes. It relies on the principle that certain isotopes of elements are unstable and undergo radioactive decay at a constant rate over time.

Is the earth approximately four billion years old? This figure was not established by radiometric dating of the earth itself. Most people are not aware of this.

Accurate radioisotope age determinations require that the decay constants (half-lives) of the parent radionuclides be precisely known and constant. However, as Dr. Snelling has written about in other articles, Uranium decay constants are not accurately known due to wide decay differences in the U isotope ratio in minerals and rocks which had been assumed to be constant by conventional geologists. Additionally, the creationist 1997–2005 RATE (Radioisotopes and the Age of The Earth) project successfully pointed out some of the pitfalls in the radioisotope dating methods, and especially in demonstrating that radioisotope decay rates have not always been constant at today's measured rates but have had a period of accelerated nuclear decay (during the global flood of Noah's day).

The general formula for radiometric dating, which encompasses various radioactive isotopes and their decay processes, can be expressed as:

$$t = \frac{1}{\lambda} \cdot \ln\left(\frac{N_0}{N}\right)$$

Where:

- t is the age of the sample in years.
- λ is the decay constant specific to the radioactive isotope being used for dating.
- N_0 is the initial amount of the parent isotope in the sample.
- N is the amount of the parent isotope remaining in the sample at the time of measurement.

The above formula is a generic representation and can be adapted to different radiometric dating methods by substituting the appropriate decay constant (λ), initial parent isotope amount (N_0), and measured parent isotope amount (N).

Uranium-Lead Dating:

- For uranium-238 (U-238) decaying into lead-206 (Pb-206):

$$t = \frac{1}{\lambda} \cdot \ln\left(\frac{N_{Pb_2 06}}{N_{U_2 38}}\right)$$

In each case, the decay constant (λ) is specific to the particular radioactive isotope and is usually determined through laboratory experiments. The initial amount of parent isotope (N_0) is typically estimated based on the assumption of the sample's formation conditions and geological context. The above formula is a generic representation and can be adapted to different radiometric dating methods by substituting the appropriate decay

Radiometric dating, particularly carbon dating, does rely on certain assumptions. Let us break down the key assumptions and discuss their implications:

Decay Rate: The decay rates of radioactive isotopes are indeed assumed to be constant over time. This assumption is based on extensive laboratory experiments that have not shown any significant variation in decay rates under normal conditions.

However, it is essential to note that extreme conditions like those found in supernovae or high-energy environments could potentially affect decay rates, but these conditions are not relevant to Earth-based dating methods.

Initial Amount of Parent and Daughter Elements: Radiometric dating methods require knowing the initial amounts of the parent radioactive element and its daughter product. For example, in uranium- lead dating, scientists need to know the initial amount of uranium and the amount of lead present when the rock formed.

This assumption is generally based on the understanding of how these elements are incorporated into rocks during their formation processes.

Inherited Daughter Isotopes: Some samples may contain "inherited" daughter isotopes that were present before the material formed. This can affect age calculations and requires careful consideration during analysis.

Contamination: To obtain accurate dates, scientists must ensure that the sample has not been contaminated by external sources of the parent or daughter elements. Contamination can lead to inaccurate age determinations. Various techniques such as sample preparation, analysis of multiple samples, and thorough examination of the geological context are employed to minimize contamination risks.

It is true that dating rocks of known ages is an important aspect of validating radiometric dating methods. For instance, dating volcanic rocks from eruptions with historically documented ages helps calibrate the technique. However, it is crucial to note that inflated ages can result from factors other than the fundamental principles of radiometric dating.

These factors might include contamination, improper sample handling, or the presence of inherited daughter isotopes.

While radiometric dating has its limitations and potential sources of error, it remains a valuable tool in determining geological ages when used appropriately and in conjunction with other dating methods and geological observations. Scientists are continuously refining these techniques and improving their understanding of the Earth's history.

Radiocarbon dating can tell you the age of the material used for the manuscript, but not necessarily the exact date when the text was written. For example, a manuscript might have been written on old parchment or reused materials..

The 'days' (Yom) referred in Hebrew have collective meanings including a literal 24-hour period or a symbolic representation of a longer time span. For interpreting biblical dates, scholars often use a combination of historical, linguistic, and archaeological evidence, rather than relying solely on radiocarbon dating. Radiometric analysis, particularly radiocarbon dating, is a valuable tool for dating manuscripts and understanding the historical contexts of biblical times. However, it is not designed to address theological questions about the creation date itself. Instead, it provides a scientific framework for understanding the age of materials and artifacts, which can complement historical and theological studies.

https://answersingenesis.org/geology/radiometric-dating/
https://answersingenesis.org/geology/radiometric-dating/u-pb-radioisotope- dating-method-problems/

Chapter 10
Objective Morality

Rape of a woman is absolutely wrong. Murder of a small innocent child is evil. We have a conscience that quickly tells us that rape is wrong and murdering a child is profoundly evil. There is an inherent sense of moral obligation and an oughtness in recognizing these acts as wrong and evil.

Stealing anyone's backpack is always wrong because every individual is a human being created in the image of God.. This divine creation bestows dignity upon each individual. Respecting someone's dignity means respecting their property, and therefore, not taking what belongs to them.

Objective morality inherent in us, is a God-given trait that we possess. For an Atheist, morality is relative, his worldview does not support objective morality. According to his worldview, humanity is merely matter that emerged from primordial sludge. However, despite this perspective, his actions and experiences reflect a commitment to objective morality. An atheist claims that objective morality comes from society, upbringing, cultures and laws.. Yet all these are relative because it depends on factors that vary since it is regulated and formed by men. When an African barbarian eats a man, he does not think it is evil, but we cannot say that is good. For the African cannibal, their sense of cultural goodness and laws is what they rely on, and it is what he considers to be good. But murdering and eating a man, we all know is always objectively evil.

Right and wrong are decided by society-

An Illustration, Nuremberg trials 1945 to 1949, twenty-four Nazi war criminals are defended by Nazi lawyers. The Nazi lawyers informed the judges at the Nuremberg trial, you have no right to condemn these Nazi war criminals because they simply were carrying out orders. They simply were doing what their culture taught them to do. The trial shut down because those brilliant Nazi lawyers were onto something. If it is true, that culture defines right and wrong, there is no way for the Allies to judge the Nazi war criminals because it was their culture who taught them that the Holocaust was good, and they were just following orders.

Robert Jackson the counsel for the American contingent, stood up and said there is a law above their Nazi law. And because of the law above their law, we can judge these Nazi war criminals as doing something wrong and the trial continued, and those 24 Nazi war criminals were judged.

If there exists a mind prior to the human mind that creates and defines right and wrong, then we can rely on our conscience and reason.

There can be a law above the cultural law, if there is some type of God who creates and defines that value of justice by His law.

Question: I'm somehow going to arrive at this natural law being correct and how is that different, if I'm saying that is simply my reason dictating. What I decided to be just and not necessarily written by God ?

Answer: Well, you can do that, but I don't think you can live it out. Because if you're gonna live out what you say, you believe, you're gonna have to acknowledge that if I steal his backpack or if I make a racial slur against you, that's not wrong in any absolute sense. Maybe it's wrong from your perspective but obviously from my perspective it's right. So your moral relativism crosses you out of the picture when it comes to making an objective moral decision as everything's relative.

Q : So, for the existence of God, you make an argument from morality. It is not actually an argument for the existence of a god, it is the argument for the fact that we should have an idea of an existence of a God because otherwise there would be no moral basis from which we could sit on. And I disagree with that because I feel that humans are inherently altruistic and moral.

A: Okay all right stop there for just a second. What do you mean by altruistic and moral?

Q: We are giving and we care about each other

A: Why is that good?

Q: Why is that good, because it helps our species survive …

65

A: Why is it good to survive?

Q: Because then we can propagate and move on as a species and continue to exist so

A: Why is that a good thing, who said?

Q: Why is that a good thing yeah, because that is what it is.

A: Well that's an is, that's not an ought though. Stalin would say, 'Find Mr X, I am going to survive by killing him and taking his stuff, 'why is he wrong ?

Q: Because Stalin would have the initial urge not to, he would feel that the inherent urge of humans is to be caring for one another. There are situations where humans will not be caring about one another and those are exceptional but because humans are inherently altruistic his first urge would be to take care of the person or try and help them but if he has some motivation against that, then he would no longer have that urge and he would decide that he wants to kill them, because he has a reason to.

A: Well again, you're I think, begging the question as to what altruism is? Why is taking care of others a good thing if there is no God, that's your opinion, Is there an external reference and authoritative unchanging reference that you're getting that opinion from, which makes it objective or is it just something you feel?

Q: Humans, um..,so if you take it from the stance that this is something that is consistent throughout humanity that we care about one another, then we could superpose that as a moral impulse that we have ….

A: Okay let me agree with you, I think we do have a moral impulse and that's exactly what C.S Lewis said in the 'Abolition of man', when he looked at all the diverse cultures and he said they agree on basic morality. Now how do you explain that basic morality. Well there may be different ways to explain it, but some will say that is because God has written it on our hearts, but the issue is not how we know it, the issue is, why is altruism as you put it or caring for one another a good thing. Who said…….

Q: It's not necessarily let who said, it is what is, we are altruistic. There is no need for someone to say that it is a good thing, it is what we are.

A: But if Hitler or Stalin comes along and says, "I don't want to be altruistic, I want to be selfish and take everything for myself and if I have to kill you to do that, I'm going to do that." Why is that objectively wrong ?

Q: Because he is not taking care of other people who said it's ……..

A: Where are you getting this standard to objective, this objective standard that you ought to take care of people. Where does that come from, if there's no God …………..

Q: I would like to share a brief example and make a few points. Firstly, our continued existence depends on our ability to care for one another. As a social species, if we didn't support each other, our chances of survival would be significantly diminished. We need to unite, support one another, and maintain friendliness.

A: That's presupposing that survival is a good thing. Why is survival considered good and valuable? Why should we prioritize human survival as good over that of cockroaches, antelopes, or black widow spiders?

Q: Why do you need the concept of good there, we are still surviving and we are being nice, kind to each other, we are being caring for one another.

A: Forgive me friend, but it seems you're borrowing the concept of goodness from a divine framework to support your worldview. If there is no objective moral standard beyond human perspective, then atheism struggles to provide a coherent basis for morality.

Q: You know I think you're right, there is something to that, the idea of Good and Evil, is in a lot of ways a religious concept.. but why do we need that.

A: It depends on what you mean by 'religion,' which can be a loaded term. Let's set religion aside and just talk about the source. Ontologically, or the study of being, where does morality originate from? Are you an Atheist?

Q: Yes ….

A: Okay, Are you a materialist?

Q: No ….

A: Okay, so you believe in the immaterial reality. That's good, how do you explain immaterial reality if there is no God..?

Q: Could you define immaterial reality ?

A: Oh, lets just take the laws of morality. It's right to take care of people, it's right to love, it's wrong to murder, where does that come from?

Q: That's something that is ingrained in us, in our behaviors ....

A: That's how we know it. Let me agree with you that maybe there are different ways we can come to know it. If evolution is true, maybe evolution has helped bring it to us. Maybe our parents taught it to us. Maybe Society taught it to us. However my question is not how we know it, my question is, why is it right to love and wrong to murder objectively. Because you know, we went to the Nazis and they said, oh we're just obeying our government. We said you had a higher obligation, to obey the good, rather than your government and you failed, so you're guilty. So where does this higher standard come from? Where does it come from, what is it ontologically ....

Q: So to some extent, this is an interpretation of.. and I'm probably going to screw this up but this is an interpretation of, why we exist and so we come from a long lineage of life and so in order to honor that, we must continue to live and so to be kind, is to honor that life that we have and life is all that we have .

A: Okay, okay, I agree with what you're saying here, but you're importing terms moral terms like honor and good into an atheistic system that has no way to ground those moral terms, that's my point.

How can matter, evolved from primordial scum and biochemical processes, account for metaphysical aspects such as truth, love, hope, and conscience? A materialistic and naturalistic worldview lacks a foundation for objective truth because it relies on personal bias and prejudice, making truth inherently relative. Yet, in practice, we live our lives grounded in objective truth, applying it to our specific circumstances. We make decisions based on a sense of right and wrong, believing certain actions (like honesty or kindness) are inherently good, and others (like theft or harm) are inherently wrong. These moral judgments imply an objective standard that transcends individual opinions or cultural norms.

Chapter 11
Transhuman — Artificial Intelligence

Transhumanists generally support the ethical use of technology to push the boundaries of what it means to be human, aspiring to create a future where humans can transcend their biological limitations and achieve greater well-being. But we have a soul, spirit and body. AI's constraints encompass the absence of emotional depth, objective morality, consciousness, spiritual understanding, and the concepts of physical and eternal mortality. We have been created in the image and likeness of God. A human newborn baby represents an extraordinary blend of biological systems, which machines can grasp analytically but cannot comprehend the profound nature of our creation as fearfully and wonderfully made by a God through the mutual love of a man and woman, both physically and spiritually.

"For You created my inmost being; You knit me together in my mother's womb. I praise You because I am fearfully and wonderfully made; Your works are wonderful, I know that full well." (Psalm 139:13-14,NIV).

AI, AGI..aim to transcend human life – an excerpt from John C Lennox,

'Transhumanists and I say guys, I respect what you're after but you're too late. And they say, what too late,of course we're not too late. I say you actually are too late.Take your two problems one physical death, I said. I believe there's powerful evidence that, that was solved 20 centuries ago it was actually solved before that but 20 centuries ago. There was a resurrection in Jerusalem, we celebrated with Easter. We're just after Easter night and as a scientist, I believe it for various reasons that we can discuss. But the point is that, if Jesus Christ broke the death barrier that puts everything in a different light. why? Because it affects you and me. How does it affect you and me. Because if that is the case then we need to recalibrate and take seriously his claim to be God became human. I said, isn't that interesting what are you trying to do, you're trying to turn humans into Gods. The Christian message goes in the exact opposite direction it tells us of a God who became human. Do you notice the difference. And of

course that actually gets people fascinated. I say you are actually taking seriously the idea that humans can turn themselves into Gods by technology and so on. Why won't you take seriously the idea that there is a God who became human, is that any more difficult to do. And once you've got that then I think arguably you need to take seriously what Jesus says. And what he says, is the Christian message, he is God become human in order to do what.. is give us his life. If you like to turn us into what you want to be because the amazing thing about this is that, the central message of the Christian faith to you and me ..is the answer to the transhumanist dream. One, Christ promises eternal life, that is life that will never cease and it begins now. Not in some mystical transhuman uncertain future but right now. Secondly because he rose from the dead he promises that we will one day be raised from the dead to live with him in another transcendent realm, that's perhaps even more real, probably more real. It is more real than this one and that's going to be the biggest uploading ever, you see. So your hope for the future of humanity changing human beings into something more desirable, living forever and happier, all of that is offered. But the difference between the two is radical. Because firstly your idea is using human intelligence to turn humans into gods bypassing the problem of moral evil, you're never going to do it. No Utopia has ever been built and of course you're not thinking straight because there have been attempts to re-engineer humanity crude. Of course.. the Nazi program of eugenics the Soviet attempts to make a new man and what do they lead to .? ...rivers of blood, 20th century being the bloodiest Century in history, mind you. What's happening now might make this a very bloody Century. I believe even more strongly than ever that, we've got as Christians a brilliant answer and a message to speak into this, that crosses all the boxes. But it means facing moral reality which is exactly at the heart of the scariness with which some people approach these issues.'

I have a friend named Sinil Andrews, who graduated with me at Engineering college,1995 . Tragically, he became bedridden after a severe accident in which he hit his back on an underwater rock while diving into a river. He suffered a rupture to the nerve in his spine, resulting in paralysis of his lower body. His parents had been his primary support for daily needs. Adding to his distress, a few years later he lost both parents, leaving him utterly alone. Despite this, I have witnessed the extraordinary way God has intervened in his life. When all hope and meaning seemed lost, God provided him with new hope and a positive outlook. His profound testimony of encountering God is so overwhelming that it compels us, as ordinary human beings, to reflect on our own understanding of life and its meaning. For the past 25 years, he has been bedridden, yet I have never heard a negative word from him. Instead, he always exudes confidence and a smile, consistently choosing to testify about the God in his life. I can see the ways, God is working in his life through the support and actions of many friends and relatives. Though his body remains lifeless below his stomach, I can see a greater life at work within his being. A life beyond human understanding. This is what God can deposit in us too.

AI or any transhuman wisdom cannot fully comprehend or explain personal, subjective experiences such as emotions, consciousness, and the sense of self. These experiences are deeply personal and often beyond the realm of data-driven analysis. The quest for meaning and purpose in life is a deeply philosophical and existential pursuit, AI cannot provide a definitive answer to what gives individual life meaning and purpose. Sinil in his own intuitive experience when he was sinking under water, started chanting the Lord's prayer expecting to die at that moment. He was carried onto a shore and from there on he was rescued and admitted at a hospital. All along, he could feel a warmth and presence of God guiding him till the hospital .

Spiritual encounters, mystical experiences, and moments of divine revelation are deeply personal and often defy logical explanation. AI or any transhuman reality cannot capture the essence of what these experiences feel like to those who undergo them. Sinil began reading the Bible and found spiritual strength as he progressed. He felt enveloped by the presence of God. Despite his own struggles, he was a source of strength for his mother, who was often overwhelmed with tears and worries.

AI lacks the ability to experience empathy and moral reasoning in the same way humans do. Creative artists are also concerned about this new incursion of AI into the realms of art and creativity. When artists create based on their valuable life experiences and God-given authenticity, their talents transport us to a realm of joy and brilliance beyond this world. True creativity involves spontaneity and originality, elements that AI cannot genuinely replicate.

Immediately after the accident, while he was in the hospital, something like an oracle occurred. He was admitted to the ICU with his lungs filled with mucus, making it difficult to breathe, and the medications were ineffective. As he felt his breathing stop and a wave of sleepiness overcame him, the doctors started hitting his chest to help him take in small amounts of air. Doctors informed his parents that he did not have much time left and, despite their best efforts to infuse oxygen, it was not helping. As Sinil slipped into a sleep-like state, he saw a brilliance of light inside him and heard beautiful songs. The ICU was on the third floor of a thirteen-story hospital. While in his sleep-like state, he found himself on an upper floor, lying on the sunshade outside the building - a kind of out of body experience. And while lying on the sunshade, from the room above him, he saw a brilliance of a light emitting from a closed window and huge harmonious sound of clapping and singing. He could not remember the lyrics of the songs. He was lying on the sunshade in such a way that, if he moved, he would fall from the building into the darkness. It was like an oracle in Sinil's inner spirit. He clearly heard a single line from the song in his native Malayalam: "the angel of death has passed me by." However, he never felt that he would die, so he could not understand why the song mentioned his death. He wanted to enter that brightly lit room but could not, as he felt he was lying on the sunshade. When the nurses woke him from his sleep, he realized he was in the ICU, and they were taking care of his breathing. Death never occurred in his mind.

This oracle-like insight does not just reveal surface feelings but delves into the core of who Sinil truly is — the essence, motivations, and the intricacies of the soul. A message from a divine source that illuminates the innermost self. How could one explain these things with matters through the physical world?

Furthermore, transhumanist approaches could go beyond mere observation, potentially offering interventions or enhancements that aid in understanding and optimizing one's inner self. This could include techniques for emotional regulation, cognitive enhancement therapies, or even technologies that facilitate deep introspection and self-discovery. These technologies could include advanced neural interfaces, artificial intelligence algorithms capable of interpreting subconscious thoughts and emotions, or even bio-enhancements that augment cognitive abilities to perceive and understand human emotions and motivations at a heightened level. Thus, transhumanism could redefine "an oracle of Sinil's inner spirit" by offering sophisticated tools and methodologies to explore and understand human consciousness and identity in ways previously unimaginable, potentially bridging the gap between the mundane and the profound aspects of individual existence.

But one thing transhumanists cannot find is the true Origin, Meaning and Purpose of this oracle — aspects that transcend their frameworks. That is the fact or metaphysical reality they cannot define. Additionally, understanding how these oracles connect to one's future life remains elusive. The God of the Bible has been communicating with men from the beginning of creation at different dispensations of time through Oracles, His Word, Miracles, Revelations and Prophecies with clarity and purpose.

After seven years, two ministers from a Pentecostal fellowship, a husband and wife were preaching the gospel on the street outside his home at Janatha-Vytilla, Kochi district in the state of Kerala, India. Sinil and his mother were keenly listening. His mother could not stop herself; she hurried out to hear the preaching of Christ. Two days later, Br. Abey Abraham and Sister Sally, the couple, came to his house asking for a Thomas and Annamma. They said the Lord had given them these names and sent them to this place to preach the gospel to a certain Thomas and Annamma. Sinil's mother was Annamma Thomas. They heard the gospel and received the salvation of Christ.

A fellowship of six people from the Sharon church came to his house, few days later. Lying in his room, Sinil could hear their singing and clapping from the hall room. The clapping and singing were in such perfect unity and harmony that it sounded like a single, cohesive sound. It was loud, clear, and beautifully unified. The clapping echoed as though it originated from a massive audience rather than just six individuals. The decibels seemed beyond what six men alone could generate. This time, he heard again the same old one line from the song clearly: "the angel of death has passed me by." The synchronisation was perfect and heavenly. He never realized which song it was, but now he got to hear the full song. It goes like this in English translation...

'All my sorrows are over.
The angel of death has passed me by.
By the precious gift of the blood of the Lamb, I was hidden and saved at that moment.
My strength and my song, Hallelujah, Jesus is my salvation.'

From that day forward, Sinil experienced a profound renewal of life. Such an intense transformation cannot be attributed to anything in the physical world; only something supernatural and personal can provide this level of peace and fulfillment. Something glorious has overshadowed his worries and pain. Luke 1: 35, *"And the angel answered her, "The Holy Spirit will come upon you, and the **power of the Most High will overshadow you**; therefore the child to be born will be called holy— the Son of God."*

Sinil Andrews resides now in Kottayam, a district in the state of Kerala, India, where he lives joyfully at Asha Kiran Palliative Care, surrounded by the love and support of his classmates from M.A. College of Engineering and his well wishers in that area. He dedicates most of his time studying and reading the word of God, embracing his divine purpose as a human. He seamlessly integrates transhuman technology into his daily routine, attending study classes via cyber platforms. This involves using meditation apps, joining online religious communities, and accessing digital versions of sacred texts, achieving a harmonious blend of technology and spirituality.

It is the love of God, expressed through the hearts of many, that sustains him. I see the providence of a heavenly, loving Father who extends His righteous right hand at just the right moment.

Sinil dreams of standing one day,

In Heavenly Father's radiant array.

Crowned with righteousness, shining bright,

All afflictions turned into a piece of art, in that new heaven, a splendid sight.

Each piece a glow, a star so fine,

Brilliance forever, a light divine.

For now, Sinil whispers, His grace suffice,

In this temporal life, offering his body as a living sacrifice.

Holy and pleasing to the Lord,

Not conformed by the world's pattern, but by His word transformed.

Glory to God, an epitome so grand,

Reigning in life, despite weakness' at hand.

In every trial, His strength reveals,

A life of Glory, His grace heals.

"Cast your burden on the LORD, and he will sustain you; he will never permit the righteous to be moved." Psalms 55: 22

Chapter 12

What Is Bible ?

I urge all my readers to explore the truth by reading the sacred texts of major religions. Often, believers rely solely on the teachings of their leaders and preachers without reading into their religious scriptures themselves. It is my sincere plea that we first familiarize ourselves with these texts before passing judgment on other believers. Instead of listening to others, take the effort of reading Holy books from at least the main line religions..

Bible is a book which contains Historical Narrative-502 chapters, Poetry- 387chapters, Discourse letters-300chapters. It is a book written over a period of over 1500 years, 40 authors inspired by the Holy Spirit, all well connected with a common purpose of revealing the same God in different dispensations of time.. It is a book that speaks to us, enlightens and relates to our existence emanating hope, faith and love.. It is the wisdom of God releasing His power into our lives…

Evidence and Proof.. Historical accounts are verified not using a scientific exercise of repeatability.. There is no proof to verify a Historical account, but we can have evidences to verify it. The Salt March event in India before India's freedom is an Historical event. It does not have proof but evidences .. We cannot prove the Salt March, but we have reliable evidence and eyewitness account for the Salt March from History ..

We have reliability of the Bible through the evidences mentioned below:-

- Eye witness account. It holds a significant value in a court of law.
- We can discern whether the text is fiction, poem or Epic when we analyse the literary style.
- Analysis of Historical narrative, We understand that it shows us the geographical and historical backgrounds.

- Archaeological evidences .. verifiable places like Bethlehem, Rome etc...These are real places and not places mentioned in a Fairy tale.
- Manuscript evidences (around Greek 5800 manuscripts written from 2CE-10CE, totally more than 25000 manuscripts from Latin and other languages).
- Internal consistency in the script. Differences in the Gospel accounts enhance their authenticity, reflecting real human interpretations—much like reporters covering the same event but reporting it in different ways. This variety adds depth and richness, rather than presenting a uniform, copied narrative.
- Character, Life, death, resurrection, words, action and works of Jesus.
- Whether Jesus is reliable? Or someone else is more reliable..?

Both the authenticity and historicity of the New Testament documents are firmly established, as vast amount of manuscript evidence is overwhelming compared to classical texts from antiquity. Original manuscripts date from within 20 to 30 years of the events of Jesus' life, that is, from contemporaries and eyewitnesses.

Historicity of these contemporary accounts of Christ' life, teaching, death, resurrection is also established on firm historical grounds. Integrity of the New Testament writers is established by their character; quality and independent nature of their witness. Secular history of 1st century and archaeological discoveries support the accuracy of their reports.

Whether Jesus is reliable ? Or someone else is more reliable..?

You are gonna live for something. I'm gonna live for something. The question is what's the evidence of whatever it is you're living for is reliable.

You are either a materialist or a hedonist or a Buddhist, a Muslim, a Jew, a Christian, an agnostic and atheist whatever you are, yeah, you are not living in a vacuum you live for something, you are motivated. So, what is the evidence that whatever it is you are living for is reliable. Every sensible human being has a world view. Your religion could be the daily morning newspaper or it could be your own self....I am standing here saying, the evidence is that Jesus Christ is reliable in a way that none of the options are. I cannot prove Christ, I cannot empirically prove Christ, but the historical evidence is, He is reliable. My observation of life is, that His analysis of life is spot-on, the existential questions that I have about significance in life, meaning and purpose in life, evil and good, hope for life after death are met in an incredible way by Jesus Christ. So, the evidence is – He Is reliable. Origin, meaning, morality and destiny..are the questions we need to ask in search of Truth ...Whatever your worldview is, it should answer these

4 questions in a corresponding and coherent way... Our final chapter in this book shows how Jesus Christ could answer these four questions in a coherent manner.

What is Bible?

Bible is not a bunch of fairy tales, but it is also not a science textbook, there is poetry, symbolic literature, history. Hinduism its mythology, now if I say to you that, I cannot accept the Gita, Vedas and Upanishads, cause its mythology. Then I lack understanding, you can communicate truth through mythology, its legitimate … I have got to dig deeper and understand it, does the evidence support the avatars of Hinduism and the whole Hindu worldview. For me to reject Hinduism, because it is claiming to communicate truth through myth, I am a narrow-minded bigot... To prove another religion is not correct, cannot be done. I could never prove God exists. Its not about proving.. the question is what is most reasonable to believe in light of the evidence. See we all have a worldview and what is the proof that you are living for is true? You would see people stumble over it … None of us can prove that our world view is correct …

A materialist viewpoint emphasizes that the fundamental principle is matter and material possessions. Therefore, it follows logically that if you are a materialist, you would prioritize living for money. There is no necessity to do so, but the principle revolves around valuing money, expensive toys, and gadgets.

What does the pantheist say? The pantheist says nature is God- you are God, so therefore meditate and get in touch with the deity that you are and the deity in the tree, that's a faith and world view ..

I cannot accept some of their truths like monism which is the belief that everything is God as being true to my life observation. Here is why I feel its not true.. If I walk up to my wife, haul back and slap her. What just happened? If I were to say, "Please accept it; it's just part of God slapping part of God." Which means you wipe out the basis of understanding of justice. She is not part of God, I am not part of God. God is a separate being who gave her value, worth and who created a value of justice. When I hold back and slap her, that is evil because I am violating a human, given worth by God. Now that is life as I experience it, that is why I think the evidence is that Christ was in touch with reality; when He talked, what He did makes sense. I live in a culture that teaches me all religions are equally valid; that is impossible for me to accept because of the Law of Non-contradiction. A and Non-A cannot both be true in the same way at the same time.

I understand that the caste system is wrong from the Sermon on the Mount. It affects the existence of your fellow men, who are also made in the likeness and image of God.. It is an Objective moral value. Empiricists assert that Ultimate reality is confined to what can be perceived through the senses—seeing, smelling, tasting, hearing, and touching. They adopt a stance of "I will believe it when I can verify it." However, this worldview cannot be conclusively proven. The empiricist viewpoint encounters limitations in proving its worldview because not all aspects of reality are directly accessible or verifiable through sensory experience alone. Concepts such as emotions, abstract ideas, and certain scientific principles may not be tangible in a way that can be perceived solely through the senses. This leads to a gap in empiricism's ability to comprehensively explain all aspects of existence, prompting questions about its absolute validity. Love is an intangible aspect of our life..

Love is often described as an intangible experience because it is not something that can be directly touched or measured in a physical sense. It encompasses emotional, psychological, and social aspects that are felt and expressed in various ways. While love may not have a tangible form like a physical object, its effects and influence can be profoundly real and impactful in people.

Obviously the biological Darwinist has profound faith that biology is the bottom line and that be it your religion, be it your ethics, be it your love or whatever. It all has a biological root. Okay, I'm a follower of Christ, I might believe there's a God who created all of this, that is my worldview and it informs me why I have my rational mind, because it is a gift from a rational creator. It informs me why life exists, because life comes from life, not from non-life. It informs me that the moral absolutes, that I am convinced are real. Like if someone picks up a gun and shoots you because you are of a different race, that is absolutely evil because it is a violation of your worth as a person. It is a violation of the value of justice. I am convinced that faith in Christ makes the most sense of life as we experience it. But everybody has faith and so the question is, what is the evidence that your faith is right, it is true. But I am really obviously frustrated with people who say, oh you religious people you have faith, the rest of us we really use logic and we really think. Excuse me! you arrogant man !! I can promise you there are many devout Hindus, Buddhists, Jews, Christians and Muslims who really think !! The question is why do you embrace the worldview you do, because none of us can prove that our worldview is true. You can't prove it, the question is, does the evidence point to your worldview being true.

Some people criticize the Bible as representing a viewpoint shaped by the Roman Catholic Church or the Nicene Council. The accepted manuscripts were recognized by early churches worldwide by around 200 AD. The early churches employed three criteria to determine the canon:

1. Authorship: Was the text written by an apostle, an eyewitness, or someone who knew an eyewitness?

2. Consistency with Tradition: Did it align with the Oral traditions passed down by the apostles and the orthodoxy of the Old Testament? This is why the Gnostic Gospels were excluded; they contradict the Genesis account of God creating the physical world and often focussed solely on inner knowledge, deeming the body irrelevant, which is considered incorrect and false.

3. Widespread Use: Was the text used universally across the known world, or was it limited to specific regions like Antioch, Jerusalem, Rome, and Alexandria?

These criteria helped ensure the integrity and consistency of the biblical canon.

Q: **Miracles, when I have no evidence for that today?**

A: If it happened all the time we might not call it a miracle, sure. Right so, we got to remember that the gospels are like ESPN sports channel highlights. The Bible does not say the miracles happened very often or every 5 minutes. Rather the gospels are sort of the highlights... occurred in the period of 1500 years.

Q: **But ESPN has video recordings unlike these Miracles?**

A: At universities, we have a department of History, where historical knowledge is a legitimate form of knowledge. And it is not based on having it on video, it's based on the reliability of eyewitness testimony. Somebody saw Abraham Lincoln assassinated by John Wilkes Booth, they wrote it down. You are paying fees to learn those historical information at colleges. It's a valid truth.

Q: **But a bullet passing to the head of another man is easy to believe, but someone descending from heaven and doing miracles is a different case?**

A: You're obviously then getting to a philosophical issue, where there is a supernatural God, in which case miracles are possible or Is there no supernatural God, in which case obviously miracles are impossible. If you allow for the existence of a supernatural God, then miracles are not irrational. Miracles are simply the supernatural God, who created the natural order choosing to change that natural order and perform what you and I call a miracle.

And when you bump up against Jesus Christ, you will notice that this is not simply a philosophical or ethical discussion that Christ engages us in. He makes some incredible claims to be God in human form, to be the resurrection of the life and then He says, " *And by the way guys, I'm going to die and rise from the dead.*" Now if He didn't rise from the dead, He is a liar because He said He was going to. If He does rise from the dead then the evidence is, you and I should trust Him.

So that is why you have got to put together some tests that you use to determine historical reliability to ascertain whether those gospels are mythology fiction or whether they're non-fiction. Historical narrative sure but I guess, whether or not the bible is historically accurate I mean, that seems to be something, that lots of people disagree about. It is something that people have devoted their entire life to proving or disproving and still everybody is throwing their hands up in the air not knowing whether or not it is true.

What year do we live in?

2024 years after the birth of Christ. Do you really think that a large number of educated people question the historicity of Jesus of Nazareth as a real person? uh no, I think most people believe that He was a person right. Okay, so there is overwhelming historical evidence that Jesus really lived, now obviously the hard question is, did he really rise from the dead?

Now watch out for your philosophical presupposition because if your philosophical presupposition is there's no supernatural God therefore miracles don't happen then of course, Christ didn't rise from the dead sure.

Q: That's not my presupposition, right good.

A: Okay, so you're open to the possibility that He rose from the dead, so put together some tests that you use to determine historical reliability. The tests that i use are four in number

First test, i ask is :- How many manuscripts do we have of the document.

You know we've Played Chinese whisper, by the time the secret reaches the end of the circle, it's totally perverted but that's not how we have the gospels. Today the gospels that we have in english are based on over 5000 copies of Greek manuscripts or pieces of manuscript, eight thousand latin manuscripts, translated by Jerome in the fifth century. Thousands of manuscripts from Coptic Aramian translators, so we have a plethora of manuscripts of the new testament all agreeing to a infinitesimal degree.

What do we have for Aristotle, Plato, Caesar, Tacitus, Lucydides, Herodotus? At the most twenty manuscripts for a particular work of theirs but for the new testament over five thousand, doesn't mean it's true but what it does mean is, we gotta take this thing seriously because the manuscript evidence is overwhelmingly supporting its reliability.

Q: Things in Herodotus, we don't take seriously, there's lots of uh supernatural stuff in the things that he recounts, most people don't believe in those things right ?

A: Right, even not christians because it's Greek myth. Correct because the literary style is mythology but when you study the new testament gospels, you will realize the literary style is not mythology, it's historical narrative. It reads like the New york times or the LA times. Let me give you a quick example of what i'm talking about, Luke chapter 3, beginning at verse 1, "In the 15th year of the reign of Tiberius Caesar when Pontius Pilate was governor of Judea, Herod Tetrarch of Galilee, his brother Philip Tetrarch of Itaria and Trekonitus and Lysanias Tetrarch of Abilene during the high priesthood of Anas and Caiaphas, the word of God came to John. To tell you the truth sir, I could give a rip about who was tetrarch and who was governor but what you can't mistake is the literary style, it is historical narrative. You go back to the roman records and you see that this guy Luke who wrote this, is a meticulous historian. He had all his tetrarchs, all his governors accurately in place. So that's the literary style, not mythology, not epic poetry like Homer's iliad or Odyssey but historical narrative, backed up with thousands of manuscripts.

Second test i use is – What's the gap between the writing of the document and the first manuscript that we have. For Aristotle, Plato, Caesar, Tacitus, Lucides, Herodotus the gap is 700 to 1400 years between the time it was written and the first manuscript that we have. The gap between the gospel of John written between 60 and 90 A.D. The first manuscript that we have located in John Ryland's university library in Manchester England is a gap of 30 to 60 years. The bodmer manuscript which contains the first 14 chapters of the gospel of John in Geneva Switzerland is dated 200 A.D. So that's 120 years after the writing, you see the gap between the writing and the extant manuscripts is so small that, we have incredibly high degree of certainty that we really have what they wrote.

Third test -within 150 years of the life of the most famous person of Jesus day, Tiberius Caesar the Roman Emperor :- how many people wrote about Tiberius Caesar - just 10. Within 150 years of the life of Christ, how many people wrote about Jesus – more than 45 non biblical sources. That's pretty impressive, this is a historical guy who really lived.

Fourth test :- When you read the gospels, look for details because if someone's lying and they give too much details. They've made a big mistake because we can check up on, for instance in the gospels, the record that, Jesus was buried not just in any tomb but in the tomb of Joseph of Arimathea. Joseph was a leader, he was a leading politician of his day. So everybody knew where the tomb of Joseph of Arimathea was and the gospel writers say, Jesus was buried in the tomb of Joseph of Arimathea. Which means, if you don't think the tomb is empty, Go and check it out, it's well known. People have been to the tomb of Joseph Aramathia, and find it's empty, with no remains of the body of christ. So it's due to those types of details, that give the gospels great credibility. So those are some of the tests that, we use to determine historical reliability. But nothing sacred about my test, if you don't like them, I'm not going to be offended but you got to come up with your own test, that you consistently use to determine what's fiction, what's non-fiction ; what's credible and what's not credible. Because if Jesus rose from the dead, man you got to put your faith in because He's the truth.

Q : Yes if it's true, i think that's right, but the point I question is whether or not it's true. Whether i have reasons to believe it's true, even if it is or whether or not it isn't. I suppose, yes it maybe the gospels are written in a narrative historical style but i think it's still a question as to whether or not they're reporting something that's true or false. I'm still….uh thinking about the fact that there are historians, experts that say that it is historically accurate and also those that say that it isn't historically accurate. For me i suppose, then i have a lot of work still to do, to go and check these things to see whether or not, they're true ! Right ? Whether they're making mistakes. It seems like, it would be a lot of work that I would have to do..?

A : Oh ! it's not that much, the gospels are about 160 pages, read them put together your test to determine historicity. Then you would be able to explain why you reject them as fiction or why you trust them as historically reliable and why you put your faith in Christ. But please don't be a cynic just saying, 'oh no, i don't believe.'

Q: Well i mean, i do feel somewhat like a cynic, i think yeah even if i do read this stuff, i'm afraid that i'm still going to be in this position where my hands are up in the air and i just really don't know.

A : Okay well if your hands are up in the air and if it's because you've done a study and the evidence is lacking, obviously the question you've got to answer is, What am i living for ? And what is the evidence that so surpasses the evidence for the reliability of Christ that i'm living for, whatever it is i'm living for. Because obviously sir you're going to have to live for something, you are right now living for something you know. You wouldn't be a student or employee wherever you are placed now, if you weren't a highly motivated person. You wouldn't be articulating as clearly and well as you do, if you hadn't put some thought into it. You're a motivated person, okay all you got to do is ask yourself, what motivates me. And whatever it is that motivates you, well that's the object of your faith. That's what you believe in, you can't prove, it's the purpose of your life. But it's you, who have chosen to say, this is worth my work, my money, my effort, i'm gonna live for this. See now you got to ask yourself, okay now why have i made that decision, what's the evidence. Because you're a skeptic, right ! so am I. What's the evidence that whatever it is you're living for is reliable ?

Q : Why should I follow a book that condones things like slavery and killing, and contains many other outdated or troubling ideas that I don't believe in? And let's put that aside, this was 2000 years ago and in this 21st century, why do i need to follow that. Give me five reasons that i need to have a religion.

A : The term "slavery" in the biblical context should not be equated with the African or Black American slavery seen in later history. In biblical times, it referred more to a form of indentured servitude, where individuals entered into a binding contract, often to pay off debts or obligations. This arrangement could last for many years and wasn't limited to unskilled labor; even highly skilled individuals, including doctors, could be bound under such agreements, often in exchange for something like passage into a country or other necessities.

You want five reasons that you need to have a religion!

Q: Yeah i'm an atheist, I don't believe in any religion and i'm a decent person. I know i have morality, i'm an ethical guy. In fact i'm more ethical than a lot of religious people.

A : I believe you.

Q: Okay so give me five reasons i need to have a religion.

A : You bet, first reason that you need to believe in Christ in God is you've got to answer, the question as a thinking human being. Where do i come from ? because that has profound implications.

Q: Where do you think i come from?

A: I think you come from God

Q: Okay, oh why should I think you're right when most of scientists don't think that way. You know if this is something that science can answer and most of scientists don't believe what you believe. I'm going to go with the scientists,who actually know what they're talking about.

A: Sir, science is a study of process right, how the organism works. Science does not answer the question like, is there an intelligent mind behind the process or is there no intelligent mind behind the process. That is a philosophical question, not a scientific question. And if any scientist stands up in class and says, i can scientifically prove that God exists, you better report his department head. Equally if somebody, if some scientist stands up in your class and says science proves that God does not exist, you better also hand him over to his department head. Science is not concerned with the question, does God exist or not, that is a philosophical theological question, right ?

Q: Let me give an example, scientists are not claiming there's a God and you guys are the people claiming there is such a such a thing. It's like i say there's a chocolate under that table. Well i'm claiming that I'm not the one who has to prove that. You're claiming there is a god so you're the one who needs to prove to me that there is a God.

A: That's another question sir. I'm trying to answer your first question and I respect you and that's why i'm trying to the best of my ability to answer your first question. You asked me to give you 5 reasons. And we'll get to the science issue, if you want to, all right but your first question was, give me five reasons, why this is important that i should believe in Christ in God. And my first point was, you have to answer the question, we all do, where do I come from ? Why..because if i'm a cosmic accident, then to argue that i have worth, value and significance is a joke. It's an exercise in futility, because if i am simply, a primordial slime evolved to a higher order, then to act like i have innate value is an exercise in fantasy. I don't have any value, i'm a cosmic accident. That's all you are, if there is no God.

Q: What do you see your value in, what's your value? so you're suggesting if i don't believe in god, i don't have any value. I don't know. What i'm doing in this planet.?

A : No, if there is no God, none of us have innate value, if in reality there is no God, we're all pond scum evolved to a higher order. Which means we don't have any innate intrinsic worth. We just exist, now we can go around saying, i am the greatest, i am the greatest but that's a fantasy, that's an illusion. Because in reality i'm not the greatest. I'm just pond scum evolved to a higher order.

Q: So are you suggesting the only reason, people do good is because of God?

A: No, that's ethics, that's different we're talking about human worth. Why is a human being valuable ?

Q : If i do good to someone, if i help someone who doesn't have food to eat, that's valuable to me, that's why i'm here. I help other people if they need help. I don't see, why you say that's not valuable, if i don't believe in god. Should i just do that because i'm scared. There's a hell and i might burn though, what do you see the value in ?

A: Listen to me sir, you're not listening. Human beings are not innately worth anything, they are pond scum evolved to a higher order now, my ex worldview. The world view of Jesus Christ is this, man is not simply pond scum involved to a higher order, He's a human being created in the image of God for a purpose. And because God has given him worth and value. He has innate value and it doesn't come from him running around saying i am the greatest, i am the greatest, i am the greatest. No it has nothing to do with that. It has to do with the fact that, he's not a cosmic accident, he's a human being created by God for a purpose..okay so that's the first reason you should seriously consider Christ.

The second reason you should seriously consider Christ is because, if atheism is True, then life is absurd, it's meaningless. And that's what atheist philosophers like Camus and Sartre and Nietzsche point out very clearly.

Sartre begins his novel, **The Stranger**, with the words of a young teenage boy who says, "*yesterday mother died or was it today, who cares when mom dies. Death simply ends the absurdity that birth began.*"

Jesus Christ says, No life is not absurd, it's not meaningless, it has a purpose. And God gave you this gift of life for the purpose of loving and worshiping God and loving and serving other people.

Third reason to consider Christ, is because you're a good atheist, you're an altruistic, moral atheist. But as Nietzsche points out - you don't have the courage to face the fact, that if you do the opposite of what you define as good, that's just as good. Because morality is relative, which means maybe you think it's good to feed the guy a meal but if you instead choose to steal his money, that's your choice, it's not evil .

Q: You're suggesting i get the morality from religions that we're hearing.

A : No, I'm saying if there is no God, morality is relative. Which means it doesn't matter whether you slit his throat or feed him dinner, it's your choice and whatever you choose is your choice, it's not good, it's not evil it's all relative, arbitrary, ephemeral right. But if there is a God, then it's possible that there's a value of justice and a value of love and you better not slit his throat. If you're able to feed him if he's hungry, you better feed him because he's hungry.

Q: First of all I was talking about religion, not God, it's the first thing I asked and so don't bring that god argument into this, that's a completely different thing here.

A : Oh you're right

Q : So I'm saying, why do i need religion. Christians claim they are best, so does Islam and other religions. Why should i follow any religion ?

A : You should not, do not follow religion. Follow Jesus Christ, not religion. Religion has been used, used to justify the crusades, the inquisition, the salem witch trials, enslaving African americans. I think you would be misguided to follow religion. Jesus Christ is totally different from religion. I would never follow religion, never. The illogical outward application of any truth or teaching does not inherently discredit the truth or teaching itself.

Q: So you would just follow a guy.

A: I would follow God. I would follow Jesus Christ. Yes sir. If you think I'm going to follow American Christianity or Asian, no way. Absolutely no way. I'd be a fool to follow American or Asian Christianity. To follow Jesus Christ that's radically different, totally different. To follow Jesus Christ has nothing to do with being a republican, has nothing to do with being a democrat or any form of human governance. It has to do with following God, following Christ. That's the bottom line, Jesus talked about the kingdom of God, the kingdom of heaven. He called people to follow him.

Q : I assume that you believe in morality. The bible are all reflections of God's essence, basically they're not arbitrary. They come from God's essential qualities. Do you believe that God is non-delimited.. meaning he's infinite. You cannot put him within certain boundaries. Describing God as beyond understanding suggests that attempting to define Him with rational constraints or labels only limits His true nature.

A : I think you have to be very very careful with that. What i mean is this, God is infinite -meaning by that specifically, he's eternal, he doesn't have a beginning or an end. He's all powerful. But that does not mean, He can make a square ..circle. It does not mean, He can make himself exist and not exist at the same time. No! We don't mean that, when we say God's all-powerful. So we have to be very careful the way we define some of those rather large concepts you've used. And when we say that God is infinite, we do not mean that he cannot step into space and time and reveal himself.

Q: The main issue i have with following exclusively one single text or religion or doctrine, is that, it's essentially a problem of putting a lot of information down into a little bit of information. For example you take a three-dimensional object like planet earth, you try to map it into two dimensions. You are gonna lose some information just because two dimensions is not as informationally rich as three dimensions. That's why I believe, divine presence, the beyond, whatever you want to call, it is so much more informationally rich, than can be put into one book or one script. So it's not that it wouldn't be valuable as a guide, a map can still be valuable but you have to be very cautious and you shouldn't just limit yourself to that one map because there could be information that's lost in the transcription of the information. Okay you know how you feel about that but that's why i can't limit myself to just say, I'm only going to believe in this religion or that religion, not try to get information. Be open to anything you know and i can't put myself under the title of one religion like, i'm a Christian, i'm a Muslim, i'm a Jew….

A: Alright, Tom, I get it. But is that acceptable, Bob? Or are you Philip? No, Josh? Okay, George. What's the problem there, the problem is not just rudeness on my part in addressing your name incorrectly, the problem is a world view that says it is impossible for me to know that you're George. And I strongly disagree with that worldview. I am convinced, i could be wrong but i am convinced that you told the truth when you told me that your name is George. Yeah and I don't think it's very wise, i don't think it's very smart and i don't think it's very intellectually honest for me to call you Tom, Bob, Philip or Josh. And then to tell you, oh by the way just chill out. You've got to allow yourself to be bigger than just George. No, if I'm going to have the privilege of getting to know George, i'm going to have to allow you to reveal to me, who you are. And if I don't allow you to reveal to me who you are, I am never going to have the privilege of a relationship with George. Now if that's true between George and me, that's obviously going to be true between God and me. I am not smart enough to figure out God that's for sure, in the same way I'm not smart enough to figure out George. God had revealed Himself through His own son Jesus Christ, in a clear, personal revelation of His character and purpose. A world view that says it is impossible for me to know

God. And I strongly disagree with that worldview. I am convinced, i could be wrong, but the manner in which the truth about God was revealed by Christ is intellectual, definitive and accessible. God is a personality and He has revealed Himself so clearly in history. Our work is to find out whether the truth is coherent and corresponding.

John 1:18:"No one has ever seen God; the only God, who is at the Father's side, he has made him known."

Hebrews 1:1–3a: "Long ago, at many times and in many ways, God spoke to our fathers by the prophets, 2 but in these last days he has spoken to us by his Son, whom he appointed the heir of all things, through whom also he created the world. 3 He is the radiance of the glory of God and the exact imprint of his nature, and he upholds the universe by the word of his power."

John 12:45: Jesus cried out " And whoever sees me sees Him who sent me.."

Chapter 13

Exclusivity - World Views

One of the most common accusations flung at Christians is that they are arrogant. "How can you believe that you're right and Hindus, Buddhists, Muslims—all the thousands of other religions—are wrong?" Isn't it the height of arrogance to claim that Jesus is the way to God? A way possibly. But The Way?

This issue haunts many Christ followers and makes us reluctant to talk about our faith. We don't want to appear arrogant, bigoted, or intolerant. This pluralistic view of religions thrives very easily in places like Canada or Europe where tolerance is valued above everything else. It's very easy slip from the true claim—'all people have equal value'—to the false claim that 'all ideas have equal merit.' But those are two very different ideas indeed.

Let's take a brief look at the **"all religions are essentially the same"** idea. Suppose I say that I've just got into literature in a big way. We have read William Shakespeare, C.S. Lewis and Tolkien, but also Harry Potter and David copperfield —and I've concluded that every author is identical. Would you conclude that: (a) *this is the most profound statement on literature you've ever heard*? Or would you conclude (b) *that I don't have firstly, a clue on what I'm talking about*? I suggest that you'd probably choose (b). Now, what about the statement *"all religions are the same"*? Doesn't it likewise suggest that the person making it hasn't actually looked into any of them? Because once you do, you realize it's not that most religions are fundamentally the same with superficial differences but the reverse is the case: ***most religions have superficial similarities with fundamental differences***.

A further problem with the idea that all religions are essentially the same is that it ignores a fundamental truth about reality: ideas have consequences. What you believe matters, because it will effect what you do. To claim that all religions are essentially the same is to say that it doesn't matter what you believe as long as you're sincere—and this neglects the fact that you can believe something sincerely and be sincerely wrong. Hitler held his beliefs with sincerity—that doesn't make them true.

However, truth, by its very nature, is exclusive. If it is true, as Christianity claims, that Jesus was crucified, died, and rose from the dead, then it is not true, as Islam claims, that Jesus never died in the first place and that somebody else was killed in his place. Both claims cannot be true. Truth is exclusive.

But just because truth is exclusive, that doesn't make truth cold and uncaring. Truth for the Christian is personal. The Jesus who said "I am the only way" also said "I am the truth." In other words, ultimate truth is not a set of propositions but a person. As the Bible says in 2 Timothy 1:12, *"I know whom I have believed."* Not what I have believed or experienced but whom I believed, Jesus Christ.

To ask why we think that Jesus Christ is the only way is to miss the point entirely. Jesus does not compete with anybody. Nobody else in history made the claims he did; nobody else in history claimed to be able to deal with the problems of the human heart like he did. Nobody else in history claimed, as he did, to be God with us. To say that we believe Jesus is the only way should have nothing to do with arrogance and everything to do with introducing people to him.

Everyone is an exclusivist. World views are Fundamentally different but superficially similar .

Pantheism.. All is God...

Christian... God is not all...

When you say Christians are excluvists...you exclude the excluvist. Bahai faith doesn't believe Jesus is the only way to God, there are many ways. Whenever you make a truth claim..you are saying the opposite is false, hence even a Bahai faith guy is also an exclusivist ...

We always hide our exclusivism under a veil of inclusivism Why?

We want to avoid the hardwork of disagreeing with each other...

Stephen Prothero says, *"No one argues that different economic systems or political regimes are one and the same. Capitalism and socialism are so self- evidently at odds that their differences hardly bear mentioning. The same goes for democracy and monarchy. Yet scholars continue to claim that religious rivals such as Hinduism and Islam, Judaism and Christianity are, by some miracle of the imagination, both essentially the same and basically good. This view resounds in the echo chamber of popular culture."*

All paths lead to God..sounds inherently respectful...

Actually its inherently disrespectful..in the way that not all paths lead to God..

Hinduism..is about self, Atman in every man..Divinity of the self. Atman is brahman.. its impersonal creative force of the universe..

Buddhism..started in rejection to Hinduism.. contrarily doesn't believe in divinity of self..It believes, we are under the illusion of selfhood. It rejects caste system...We are accretion of karma... Work of our bad karma of previous lives..Four noble truths and Eight fold path extinguishes self. You would become nothing...but Hinduism suggest your goal is to become one with divine. But Buddhism rejects the divine..and goal is to become nothing.. We see exclusivity in all worldviews...

Christian believes God is one and is triune being. One being, different persons...Father sends the Son to the world and the Son pays the debt back to the Father. That makes sense of the cross..

But Islam thinks that as blasphemous and God is one. They reject this. God would never condescend and incarnate himself and die on a cross for a Muslim...

When we say all paths are same..we are being irrational and lose all sense of wisdom..

Disagreeing is not hatred. We can agree to disagree thus respecting values and showing integrity in intelligence.

T..Total objective truth and many small t' s points towards the big T.... None of us know all of T. If I knew everthing I would be God.. Small t...they say are different religions. Which has portions of equally valid truth but incomplete versions...so we cannot disagree with each other. If so what about Hitlers, Stalins, Mao tse jungs, Idi Amins.....do we not disagree with their truth?..Of course we disagree with them...Are you sure that you cannot disagree with anyone since your version is incomplete? We can disagree with each other. Absolutely, we can and should disagree with ideologies or actions that are harmful, oppressive, or violate basic human rights, regardless of the context of incomplete understanding. Disagreement isn't solely about having a complete understanding of truth; it's also about ethical principles, empathy and a commitment to justice.

When we try to sideline Christian as an exclusivist ..we have forsaken the God given wisdom on the Altar of supposed tolerance.

Becoming too focused on acquiring all information and truth can sometimes lead Christian exclusivists to come across as arrogant in their conversations. When we aim to be well-informed and knowledgeable, it's crucial not to turn the Christian faith into a tool for trying to make others feel regretful for asking questions. Instead, let's approach discussions about faith with humility and respect, avoiding the pitfalls of turning Christian persuasion into a means of making others feel unwelcome or inadequate. 1Peter 3: 15 says that you need to deliver the message of Christ with gentleness and respect.

Analysing the Arrogance claim on Christians....

Secular humanist manifesto says : Human beings have the ability and the responsibility to lead ethical lives of personal fulfillment that aspire to the greater good of all-basically the ability inside of you ..

Gospel believes you and me are sinners and we don't have the ability to lead a perfect life. It is from God we receive the fullfillment and empowerment.- In these 2 cases ..who is arrogant?...

When we say Christians are arrogant when they claim exclusivity..thats being extremely judgmental..

If its exclusive and true at the same time.....we need to believe it..

Tolerance has lost its true meaning in this age. Tolerance is the ability to withstand in a situation of uncomfortable stress or any disagreement. Tolerance is not about agreeing with each other and ignoring the obvious differences. True tolerance is that you are willing to put up a stress..which is a beautiful thing..

Exclusivity allows us to really delve into each others depths and diversity of world views or else you would not know it...

Inclusivity breeds intellectual laziness and we lose track of truth and reality...

All world views are trying to answer the question of meaning of life ...

Secular humanism believes in objective specialness and valuable essence of human beings, where they don't need a God to justify that specialness. But the problem is that, with out God, all you are, is a result of an accidental accretion of various chemicals and processes..that makes you a complex chemical machine. How are you special then? May be you are special because of 3.1 billion bits of information in a small nano size single cell DNA strand created by God. Bible doesn't use the words..you were constructed or designed, it says you were knit in your mother's womb (Psalms 139:13-15). What do you think when you say the word knit. Knitting as all pregnant mothers and grandmothers are aware.. thats how they knit together and make a beautiful baby clothing even before the baby comes. When she was knitting it….yes there was a design and pattern..but above all, a tender loving care and intimacy while doing it...my baby, my son... Knitting implies intimacy.

Secular humanism wants to believe that somehow we are special and somehow we have value and meaning. But how can man, who they claim is a result of a blindless pitiless mindless chemical reaction in an indifferent world can assign a value....how in the world can you justify that belief ? On the other hand, if we consider ourselves as creations of a divine intelligence capable of making deliberate choices to bring us into existence and caring for us, then we can find a basis for affirming our value and purpose. True value and meaning comes through the ever loving care of our God knitting us in our mother's womb, fearfully and wonderfully made, displaying a signal of transcendence in you and me. Originated from an intimate loving God...Christ is the answer affirming the depth of our worth as beings shaped by divine love. How can we justify value if we are product of chemical process ? Only God can..

Psalms 139 : For you formed my inward parts; you knitted me together in my mother's womb.

14 I praise you, for I am fearfully and wonderfully made.Wonderful are your works; my soul knows it very well.

15 My frame was not hidden from you, when I was being made in secret, intricately woven in the depths of the earth.

In certain belief systems, it's understood that God is infinitely superior to all beings. How then can such a majestic God endure suffering on a human cross ?....But there is a Historical reality of crucifixion, a Historical reality of resurrection. THAT if GOD is truly great and superior, then the greatest possible being would exhibit the great possible ethic, which is LOVE and which He would do it in the greatest possible way... that is self sacrifice.. Cross demonstrates a great God.

Romans 5:8,NIV, *"But God demonstrates his own love for us in this: While we were still sinners, Christ died for us."*

Exclusivity of Christ is not that it excludes people but excludes falsehood... John 3:16, *"For <u>God so loved the world</u> that he gave his one and only Son, that whoever believes in him shall not perish but have eternal life"*...**Thats the most exclusive means of salvation with the most inclusive means of love towards the whole world.**

Latin word ..Crux the root word for crucifixion means point of converging and turn. Cross is the point of converging and turning for all our questions of life..The crux of all our questions is within the Calvary cross of Jesus ..God writes his poetry through means of history

1 When I survey the wondrous cross
On which the Prince of
glory died, My richest gain I
count but loss, And pour
contempt on all my pride.

2 Forbid it, Lord, that I should boast,
Save in the death of Christ my God!
All the vain things that charm me most,
I sacrifice them to His blood.

3 See from His head, His hands, His feet,
Sorrow and love flow mingled down!
Did e'er such love and sorrow meet,
Or thorns compose so rich a crown?

4 His dying crimson, like a robe,
Spreads o'er his body on the tree;
*Then I am **dead** to all the **globe**,*
*And all the **globe** is **dead** to me.*

5 Were the whole realm of nature mine,
That were a present far too small;
Love so amazing, so divine,
Demands my soul, my life, my all.   - Issac Watts,1707

The fourth stanza of this hymn, it inspires quite powerful images:
The last two lines of the stanza form a chiasmus, as hymnologist J. Richard Watson notes, "a crossing over on the manner of the Greek letter chi: It is found . . . in the great fourth verse, which takes the idea from Galatians 6:14." That's a beautiful example of a chiasmus, where the structure creates a cross-like pattern in the text. It adds a layer of visual and thematic depth to the poetry, emphasizing the central idea through its mirrored arrangement.
Gal 6: 14, " *May I never boast except in the cross of our Lord Jesus Christ, through which the **world** has been crucified to **me**, and **I** to the **world**.*"

It is now generally conceded that parallelism is the fundamental law, not only of the poetical, but even of the rhetorical and therefore of higher style in general in the Old Testament Hebrew. By parallelism in this connection is understood the regularly recurring juxtaposition of symmetrically constructed sentences. The symmetry is carried out in the substance as well as in the form, and lies chiefly in the relation of the expression to the thought. The Hebrew word יוּוּד (divuy) specifically refers to parallelism.

Given that God is an infinitely good being, and the Bible tells us that He cannot look upon sin (Habbakuk 1).

There was a point at which mankind disobeyed God and created a separation between Him and man . In Luke 16, we see that "between Us and you a great chasm has been set in place." God, being God, resides on one side of this chasm. This side is perfect and without any sort of sin whatsoever. We, on the other hand, are on the opposite side of this chasm. The only way to get across that bridge from our side to His side is to completely remove the stain of sin. Of course, this is not possible for us to do as everything on this side of the chasm is stained with sin. One cannot clean the stain with a stained cloth, as it were.

So, how do we create that bridge across the chasm? A bridge has to exist on both sides in order for it to be useful. Therefore, we needed a bridge that could exist on the human side and also on the divine side of the chasm. This is where Jesus comes in. From the beginning Jesus was the divine Son of God. He was one of the three individual persons who shared the divine essence with God the Father and the Holy

Spirit. Because of this, Jesus (as the bridge) obviously meets the criteria to be on the divine side of the chasm.

Jacob, the son of Isaac, lived almost 19 centuries before Jesus. In Jacob's dream at Bethel, he saw a ladder extending from earth to heaven. Later, Jesus referred to himself as that ladder and bridge, symbolizing the connection between heaven and earth.

Chapter 14

Similar Stories, Just God

Q: When discussing historical figures prior to Christ who shared qualities similar to those attributed to Jesus, such as dying and being resurrected. The Egyptians believed their god Horus did that and there's many other similar cases. I often turn to Thomas Aquinas' four-fold interpretation of the Old Testament. Aquinas saw certain parts of the Old Testament as prefigurations of Christ. While I believe Jesus Christ is our savior, I approach these comparisons with humility. I can't definitively say whether figures like Horus were real or not, as there are accounts resembling those of Jesus Christ, but I don't have concrete evidence to confirm or deny their existence. Do you believe in his existence ?

A: No. Horus is an ancient Egyptian deity who was worshipped as a god of the sky, kingship and protection. In Egyptian mythology, Horus is typically depicted as a falcon-headed deity or as a falcon itself. He was considered to be a symbol of divine kingship and was closely associated with the pharaoh, who was often seen as the earthly embodiment of Horus, often portrayed as the son of Osiris and Isis.

Q: No but no, but that's not my point, my point is that …. i don't think, that's the point of the Egyptian mythology, right, but yeah i think you can communicate truth through myth. But let's be honest it's myth right, i mean the Vedas and Upanishads of Hinduism, they're not claiming that this is historical, they're saying it's myth but we're communicating truth through myth.

ANS: Fine no problem, but obviously the New testament is not saying this is myth. The new testament is saying this is a historical person, Jesus of Nazareth and truth is being communicated through an historical person, so that's the difference right.

Q : Certainly, there are numerous accounts from various sources that are considered historically accurate by different individuals. For instance, Muhammad is widely regarded as a historical figure.

A: Right, well i think, if anybody says, oh no, Muhammad was a myth, they're out to lunch, the overwhelming historical evidence is Muhammad was a real person, who really lived. There's no doubt in my mind about that.

Q: Can Thomas Aquinas' method of interpretation be applied to suggest that the death and resurrection of other historical figures, who some might argue to be myths, could be seen as prefigurations of Jesus Christ?

A: No, I wouldn't do that, instead if someone comes to me and says .. 'Hey, somebody rose from the dead,' Wow, I want to study it, i want to find out. Does the evidence point that way, you know. What one of my biggest challenges is, i live in a culture filled with a lot of people who think Elvis rose from the dead and Jesus didn't. I got my work cut out, for me man… i mean, that's incredible, there is no evidence that Elvis Presley rose from the dead, there's a truckload of evidence that Jesus Christ did rise from the dead. That's why i do not believe that Elvis rose from the dead and i do believe that Jesus did rise from the dead. I don't believe in the resurrection of Horus because it's presented in a mythological context. The only account I know of that predates Christ and claims resurrection is in a mythological form, which is why I find it unconvincing. It's the Egyptian belief, that Osiris who was chopped into 14 pieces and then his sister and wife Isis goes looking for those 14 pieces, finds 13 of them. One part, she doesn't find.. you'll never guess what that part was… she uh she puts those pieces back together again. Then he resurrects to live in the underworld and gives birth to their son Horus. And then people try and really say to me, you see that's where the resurrection of Christ comes from !! You've got to be kidding me, no, yeah it's totally different, radically different and that's the only account of a resurrection that predates Christ. When people claim that Christianity borrowed elements from other religions, such as the missing resurrection theme in Osiris' myth, I see it as a conversation about shared themes and motifs in ancient myths….balony !! The account in the Gospels presents Jesus of Nazareth as a historical figure who lived a human life—eating, sleeping, teaching, and ultimately dying. The claim of his resurrection sets Christ apart, making it distinct from other similar stories in terms of its historical assertion.

Q: A common question arises about why people who lived in remote areas without contact with Jesus Christ or those who grew up in different religions without exposure to Christ may not have had the chance to hear about him. I've read Benedict Spinoza's view that Jeremiah and Moses foresaw a time when God would inscribe His law directly onto people's hearts, and this aligns with what I've been discussing. Do you think that just because someone doesn't believe in Jesus Christ as we do, it doesn't necessarily mean they're disconnected from God?

A: That's exactly right, okay..you make a great point, that's this whole objective moral argument that i've been going over and over again !! Every human being, every atheist, every agnostic, every buddhist, hindu, jew, muslim, every person on the face of the planet has a moral indicator inside called a conscience that ties them into an objective moral law. My point is that the existence of an objective moral law requires some form of God to create and define it.

Now the second issue that you raise, is a very thoughtful issue….How is God going to judge those people who've never heard about christ ?

The Bible suggests that God judges people based on the knowledge they possess. Judgment is made according to the light or understanding they have, meaning those who have never heard of Christ won't be judged for not having faith in Him, which would be unjust since they lacked the opportunity to know about Him. Rather, Paul says in Romans one and two that they will be judged on the basis of how they've responded to God's general revelation in nature and in conscience.

Paul's teachings highlight that every person, regardless of time or place in history, can recognize the existence of an eternal and powerful deity who created the world. In Romans chapter two, he emphasizes that God's moral law is ingrained in the hearts of all individuals, even those who are not familiar with the Old Testament law. This innate understanding of right and wrong guides our actions. Consequently, those who have never encountered the gospel will be judged based on their response to God's general revelation through nature and conscience. However, this doesn't imply salvation apart from Christ's work; rather, it suggests that the benefits of Christ's sacrifice can apply to someone even without their conscious knowledge of Him. If someone were to observe the world and acknowledge the existence of a Creator while also recognizing their own shortcomings in meeting God's moral standards, and if they humbly sought forgiveness and grace from this God, they would be saved through the grace and sacrifice of Christ, even without explicit knowledge of Him. This person would be akin to those in the Old Testament who lacked conscious awareness of Christ but responded positively to the light and knowledge they had, ultimately being judged based on that response.

While Jesus didn't explicitly address this question, there are points to consider. Firstly, we understand that God's nature is just, ensuring fairness for everyone.

Secondly, eternal separation from God isn't due to a mistake or lack of information.. The reason people end up separated from God for eternity, which is what hell represents, is because they choose to live their lives apart from God. God doesn't force anyone into heaven against their will. So, the theme song of hell could be "I Did It My Way," and God respects that choice without interference. Additionally, Hebrews chapter 11 in the New Testament mentions numerous individuals like Abraham, Isaac, Jacob, Moses, and Rahab—a Gentile prostitute—who likely never heard of Jesus during their time, yet they demonstrated humility and faith in God. Many individuals from diverse regions like India, Africa, North America, South America, and China will likely be in heaven despite never hearing about Christ. Their presence in heaven stems from their humble faith in God to the best of their understanding and ability. Their entry into heaven isn't based on leading a perfect life, as none of us do, but rather on God's love for them, the application of Christ's sacrifice to their lives, and His grace. This same reason applies to figures like Abraham and Moses, securing their place in heaven. Moses had a past as a murderer, and Abraham had his own significant flaws, like passing off his wife as his sister. These shortcomings show they were far from perfect. However, the key reason Abraham will be in heaven is his faith in God. God's forgiveness and grace, through Christ's sacrifice, extend to him despite his imperfections. Does that seem reasonable?

A: Yeah, no it does.

Q: I've always grappled with the idea of heaven and hell because they are portrayed as infinite states—one as a reward and the other as a punishment. However, these infinite consequences seem to be granted based on finite actions. Doesn't that raise concerns about fairness?

A: Let's imagine a scenario in kindergarten where I slap you in the sandbox because I believe you took something of mine. The teacher intervenes, and I receive a detention. Then, in a rash decision, I slap the teacher and face more serious consequences. She sends me to the Principal's office. However, the situation escalates further when I slap the Principal, and he sends me to the Police. Even more so, when I slap a police officer. This pattern continues until I reach the judge, where I'm facing significant penalties and possibly prison time. The difference in consequences from hitting you at the sandbox to hitting the judge boils down to the level of authority. As you go up the ladder of authority, the penalty level increases… Rest assured, the Judge of all the earth administers justice far more perfectly than our human systems ever could.

"Will the Judge of all the earth not do what is right?" —Genesis 18:25, NIV

Chapter 15

Why Jesus ?

This is a very difficult and almost painful thing to say, but the simple truth is that there are no good people. Human goodness is truly relative. I know that we often think of ourselves as being good people when we compare ourselves to others. *'No man knows how bad he is, till he has tried very hard to be good.'* --C.S Lewis..

Once someone came to ask Jesus and said, *"Good teacher, what must I do to inherit eternal life* ? (Luke 18:18-19). The individual sought guidance on doing good. In response, Jesus looked at him and questioned, *"Why do you call me good?"* He then continued, "No one is inherently good enough to attain heaven; only God possesses that goodness."

Think about this: If you have to be good to go to heaven and only God is good, who is going ? God alone and …. No one else. We cannot attain any divine nature in this human condition. But it had to work the other way round. The divine had to become human to redeem us from this body of sin. But all at a cost. The debt of sinner cannot be achieved by any of our goodness. It is the goodness of God (or more accurately the righteousness of God) that can clear our debt of sin. There is a legal obligation incurred when we transgress God's law.

Now sometimes we find this statement offensive.

The tragedy of human sin arises, not because we are constitutionally inferior to other creation. Human rebellion against God is a cosmic tragedy only because humans are made in the image of God, in a position of dignity and honor (Psalms 8: 5 *For thou hast made him a little lower than the angels, and hast crowned him with glory and honour.*) to have dominion over the rest of the earthly creation. Sin therefore is a broken ruptured relationship with God. Sin is defined as missing the mark.

God is an Infinite, Personal, Relational, Holy, Righteous, Non comprehensible, Non-physical(Spirit), timeless, eternal, Intelligent, Moral, Valuable, First cause. When we affirm that God is **Holy**, we're acknowledging His highest form of wisdom, which is manifested in the supreme relationship of Love within Him, within the God head of Trinity.

John 17 : 24,KJV *"Father, I will that they also, whom thou hast given me, be with me where I am; that they may behold my glory, which thou hast given me: for thou **lovedst** me before the foundation of the world."*

Indeed, the question "What is God?" leads us to understand that God is a supreme being and is One in essence, consisting of Father, Son, and Holy Spirit. However, when we ask "Who is God?" the answer speaks of His personality, depicting Him as Father, Son, and Holy Spirit. One God in three persons. The concept of God as a Trinity—Father, Son, and Holy Spirit—is beyond our earthly comprehension or dimensions. Yet, this is what the Word of God indicates.

Love is inherently relational and requires personal interaction. It cannot exist between a person and an impersonal entity because love involves emotions, intentions, and conscious decisions, which are characteristics of persons, arising from the inherent free will choice. God is not just a impersonal entity like a force or an energy. The force or energy part would only be one of his attributes. For God to have love in himself or with humans, He needs to be a person in the first place. To illustrate, if we attribute all the good sleep we had, to the breeze or wind from a fan, we are overlooking the role of the creator of that wind, which is the electric fan itself. The wind is simply an attribute or feature of the moving electric fan. God is a supreme being with a personality. God is Love, because love was always there within the Trinity of God. God didn't have to create man to experience Love. Love was already in the God head. What makes us human beings, is the capacity of free relationships, loving each other. We cannot love a impersonal being. We can love only a person or a being which has free will. Obviously we cannot love a robot. Losing our personhood is same as being without Love, even with a God. The engagement of our personality in a lasting and fulfilling relationship - and this is precisely what God has offered in Jesus Christ.

Jesus Christ the Bible teaches us, is "God of God, Light of Light, very God of very God, eternally begotten, not made, being of one substance with the Father." ETERNAL BEGOTTEN SON OF THE FATHER.

Begotten, the Greek word *Monogenes* is "pertaining to being the only one of its kind or class, unique in kind." This is the meaning that is implied in John 3:16 (see also John 1:14, 18; 3:18; 1 John 4:9). John was primarily concerned with demonstrating that Jesus is the Son of God (John 20:31), and he uses *'monogenes'* to highlight Jesus as uniquely God's Son—sharing the same divine nature as God. The rest of the humanity are adopted sons through Christ ..(Ephesians1:5).

Consider Colossians1:13-17: Just as a father's age, is as old as his firstborn son, God's role as a father spans eternity. Therefore, there must be someone who has given Him the title of Father from eternity. When we say Jesus is the "firstborn," we're not suggesting He was created but acknowledging His eternal status as the Son. Jesus existed eternally and was responsible for creating everything before the beginning of anything that was made, which is a unique attribute of God. He was eternally as Son of God, uncaused, begotten from the Father, not made.

"The Son is the radiance of God's glory and the exact representation of his being, sustaining all things by his powerful word." Hebrews 1:3,NIV serves as the biblical foundation for this understanding. In this verse, the Father is depicted as the source of radiance, while the Son radiates this light, much like the relationship between the Sun and the light it emits to reach us. The term "radiance" or "apogasma" signifies the outshining or radiance emanating from a shining object. Just as the Sun and its light share the same essence and cannot exist without each other, the Father cannot be the Father without the Son and the Spirit. This unity demonstrates that they are one being. While it may not be the perfect analogy, it does help convey the clarity of the topic being discussed.

Jesus is consistently referred to as the Word of God throughout scripture. Further examples can be found in John 1:1-4, 17, where it is stated that the source of the Word is the Father. It's inconceivable for God to exist completely and eternally without His Word; they are inseparable. Jesus has had life within Him since eternity, even before any creation, as referenced in John 5: 26 *For as the Father has life in himself, so he has granted the Son also to have life in himself.*

God is Light, there is no darkness in Him. God is the Creator and the rest of the things are all his creation. He is the only entity in existence, the reason for whose existence is in himself. God is uncaused. All other entities or quantities exists by virtue of something else. The whole universe and nature are His creations which is the physical realm we see. God is the Creator of both the Spiritual and Physical realm. *"For since the creation of the world God's invisible qualities—his eternal power and divine nature—have been clearly seen, being understood from what has been made."* Romans 1:20,NIV

When man sinned, God's Spirit was taken away from man, as God doesn't compel himself and He is a God of covenant relationship, unchanging, truthful. When Man rebelled, God's Spirit no longer resided in man. It was by one man's disobedience that a rupture was caused in the relationship with God. The relationship was also brought back and reconciled by one man as a promise given By God the Father through God the Son. Jesus is truly God and truly man at the same time. Infinite eternal God becomes finite for a purpose of redemption and mark of his love to humanity to redeem humanity by the ultimate Sacrifice on the cross. He chose to come in the nature of servant as foretold by prophets centuries back to fulfill the will of God. The Messiah..,thus God was incarnated as Man.

Philipians 2: 5-11,NIV *"In your relationships with one another, have the same mindset as Christ Jesus: Who, being in very nature God, did not consider equality with God something to be used to his own advantage; rather, **he made himself** nothing by taking the very nature of a servant, being made in human likeness. And being found in appearance as a man, he humbled himself by becoming obedient to death— even death on a cross! Therefore God exalted him to the highest place and gave him the name that is above every name, that at the name of Jesus every knee should bow, in heaven and on earth and under the earth, and every tongue acknowledge that Jesus Christ is Lord, to the glory of God the Father."*

According to God's law, bowing down or worshiping any man or angel other than God—is considered idolatry, the greatest sin and is something that God deeply detests. We see Jesus being worshipped and bowed to in scripture throughout.

Sin is vertical, inward, conditional. Sin cannot be ignored or done away with. Forgiveness has to be real.

Forgiveness must encompass both love and justice to be meaningful. Love without justice lacks a foundation for moral correctness. Justice serves as the companion of love, ensuring fairness and righteousness. God's love extends to us, but His justice also plays a crucial role. However, in the context of our sinful condition, particularly in Christianity, bridging the gap between love and justice was a unique challenge. For instance, if someone committed a heinous crime like child murder, justice demands capital punishment. Simply releasing the offender without consequence, solely as an act of love, would be unjust and would not uphold the integrity of love being displayed.

And what Gods Justice demanded, his Love provided and his love sent his son. And so that in sending his son to pay the price :- the pure for the impure, the just for the unjust, the unpayable by the one who could pay it. He comes and pays it in full, so that you and I could be offered, that bridge through his son to come back and be reconciled to the Father. So first in the Christian faith the price had to be paid. And he paid it in his son, where we are already told by the world that – 'Relationship' isn't the first entity of this world.

Life preceeds love in other world views. The world says, "To have God's Love we need to lead a Sacred life." Love preceeds Life in Christian view. Love in the trinity, and Lord offers his love. There exists a singular moment in human history where Ultimate Evil, Justice, Love, and Forgiveness converge and find a common meeting ground –At the mount of Calvary ..the Cross of Christ!! Cross signifies the epitome of evilness of men, Justice and Love of God with an emergence of his Forgiveness. The best sacrifice that God approved. A sinless man paying the wages for a sinful human race. 2 Corinthians 5: 21, *"For our sake he made him to be sin who knew no sin, so that in him we might become the righteousness of God."*

God loved us first .We love each other because God loved us first.

The Holy Spirit, as God, can dwell within each of us, and Jesus affirmed, *'My sheep hear my voice'* indicating that God's Spirit can communicate with our human spirit. Having the Holy Spirit indwelling doesn't mean we become God; rather, we become adopted children of God in the spiritual sense. Our inner being or spirit becomes the genuine child of God, transitioning from a state of slavery to sin to one of adopted sonship, inheriting spiritual riches.

In God's family, we are regarded as sons rather than slaves. However, when we were influenced by the world or the Universe, we were slaves to the prince of this world, Satan. It's crucial to be cautious when worshiping the Universe, as it can inadvertently lead to worshiping the evil one.

According to scripture, Satan is the only being besides God who attempted to elevate himself to the divine state, proclaiming, 'I am God and will reach the position of God.' He is known by various names such as Lucifer, the devil, the serpent, the morning star, and is often referred to as the Prince of the Universe or the Prince of the Air. However, his authority is temporary and doesn't extend to believers in Christ.

Satan even tried to tempt Jesus himself, offering him authority over the world. It's a striking contrast—a spiritual being like Satan attempting to tempt the Creator in human form. Jesus had to take the human nature because of many reasons which the word of God explains clearly.

God knew a time would come when men would start worshipping His creation rather than Him which was also prophesied thousands of years back.

Romans 1: 20, *"For his invisible attributes, namely, his eternal power and divine nature, have been clearly perceived, ever since the creation of the world, in the things that have been made. So they are without excuse.*

21 For although they knew God, they did not honor him as God or give thanks to him, but they became futile in their thinking, and their foolish hearts were darkened.

22 Claiming to be wise, they became fools, 23 and exchanged the glory of the immortal God for images resembling mortal man and birds and animals and creeping things."

Romans 3: 23, *"for all have sinned and fall short of the glory of God."* Sin is not just an act, it is also a condition before it becomes an act (missing the mark- sin). Malcolm Muggeridge, british journalist said, *"The depravity of man is at once the most empirically verifiable fact but at the same time the most intellectual resisted fact. The fact that they deny sin is proof of their sin, core of sin is pride. Man is morally self determining being."* He also said, *"People do not believe lies because they have to, but because they want to."* You don't have to teach a small child on how to become angry or complaining or disobedient ..

"Jesus didn't come to make bad people good. He came to make dead people live" – C.S Lewis

In our discussions, we often focus on morality, but Christ emphasized on righteousness, which differs slightly from morality. The Bible states that no one is righteous, and it's impossible to achieve righteousness through human efforts. Righteousness is an attribute exclusive to God and cannot be earned through good deeds or works. We're not comparing righteousness among people but aiming for a superior righteousness akin to God's holy and incomparable standard. The highest form of human righteousness, according to the Bible, are like filthy rags in comparison to righteousness of God.

Isaiah 64: 6- *"We have all become like one who is unclean, and all our righteous deeds are like a **polluted garment**. We all fade like a leaf, and our iniquities, like the wind, take us away."*

The pinnacle of our own righteous acts or deeds falls short when compared to God's standard of righteousness, which is nothing short of perfection. The only righteous act that God deemed worthy of entry into heaven was the Sacrifice on the Cross.

Various individuals and religions adhere to different laws or paths, each with their own texts and teachings. According to scripture, Moral Laws serve as a guide that leads us to Christ. The Law acts like a mirror, revealing the extent of our faults and shortcomings. Just as a mirror can't clean your face but only shows the dirt on it, the Law can inform and educate but cannot transform your heart. It's similar to recognizing that you need to wash your face after seeing yourself in the mirror; the Law points us to the true source of cleansing, which is found in Christ.

Let's consider how laws function with a practical example, like traffic laws. They always outline what constitutes good and bad driving behavior, but they only penalize you for the mistakes you make, never acknowledging the times you drive well. In the same way, God's law serves as a gauge of our weaknesses or sins; it doesn't inherently make us good. Just as breaking a traffic signal indicates a fault, even the smallest desires, lusts, or lies cannot be justified by God's perfect righteousness.

Without the law, we wouldn't have a clear understanding of right and wrong. Our conscience also acts as an internal law guiding us between good and bad. Overall, the purpose of the law is to help us realize that, despite any good deeds we may do, a single wrongdoing is enough to condemn us to the consequences of sin, which is spiritual death. While this may seem harsh, God provided a solution for our incapability through our acceptance of His plan. This solution, though excruciatingly painful for Him to implement through the Cross, is as simple as believing in His solution.

Galatians 3: 19,NIV *"Why, then, was the law given at all? It was added because of transgressions until the Seed to whom the promise referred had come.*

*23 Before the coming of this faith, we were held in custody under the law, locked up until the faith that was to come would be revealed. 24 So **the law was our guardian until Christ came that we might be justified by faith**. 25 Now that this faith has come, we are no longer under a guardian.*

26 So in Christ Jesus you are all children of God through faith, 27 for all of you who were baptized into Christ have clothed yourselves with Christ.28 There is neither Jew nor Gentile, neither slave nor free, nor is there male and female, for you are all one in Christ Jesus. 29 If you belong to Christ, then you are Abraham's seed, and heirs according to the promise."

God regarded Abraham's faith in Him as righteousness, a righteousness that was not achieved through Abraham's good deeds but rather through God's imputed righteousness because of his faith.

Romans4:1-5, *" What then shall we say was gained by Abraham, our forefather according to the flesh? For if Abraham was justified by works, he has something to boast about, but not before God. For what does the Scripture say? "Abraham believed God, and it was counted to him as righteousness." Now to the one who works, his wages are not counted as a gift but as his due. And to the one who does not work but believes in him who justifies the ungodly, his faith is counted as righteousness,"*

The concept in the Old Testament, as seen through Moses, serves as a foreshadowing of the revelation in the New Testament. Before introducing the Ten Commandments, the answer is provided in Exodus 20:1-3, where God speaks, "I am the Lord your God, who brought you out of the land of Egypt, out of the house of slavery. You shall have no other gods before me."

God's focus isn't solely on the commandments or righteous acts. Initially, He prioritized saving His people, symbolized by bringing them out of slavery in Egypt—an indication of God's prophetic act of redeeming us from the slavery of sin. Afterwards, He provided the law of life for them to follow and worship Him.

In this perspective, redemption comes before righteousness, which in turn leads to worship. You cannot be righteous until you have first been redeemed. It is through faith in Christ's redemptive work on the cross that you gain a right standing with God, or righteousness. Worship follows from this God imputed righteousness on you. Unlike other beliefs where salvation or redemption is the final step after you have demonstrated acts of your own righteousness and worship, here Christ's salvation comes first. He saves you initially, and as a result of this saving work, you are made righteous. This God imputed righteousness (not your own righteousness gained by doing righteous deeds) then leads to thankfulness resulting in worship of God, and ultimately to eternal life. To illustrate, first you rescue your drowning daughter, so that she can love and admire you and then she can have the opportunity to live a good life. Righteousness is the fruit and not the root. Redemption of God is the root.

Is truth Dead ? …. The work on the Cross is God's redemption (Cross of Christ). We become righteous before God when we understand that we are truly a sinner, unrighteous and repent to God and believe in God's redemption.

Colossians 2 : 9-15, NIV *"For in Christ all the fullness of the Deity lives in bodily form, and in Christ you have been brought to fullness. He is the head over every power and authority. In him you were also circumcised with a circumcision not performed by human hands. Your whole self ruled by the flesh was put off when you were circumcised by Christ, having been buried with him in baptism, in which you were also raised with him through your faith in the working of God, who raised him from the dead. When you were dead in your sins and in the uncircumcision of your flesh, God made you alive with Christ. He forgave us all our sins, having canceled the charge of our legal indebtedness, which stood against us and condemned us; he has taken it away, nailing it to the cross. And having disarmed the powers and authorities, he made a public spectacle of them, triumphing over them by the cross."*

Good works are like the fruit not the root —they should improve the community and the world around us. God has predetermined these good works for each of us before the world began. They are a reflection of our faith and should not be pursued for personal gain. If good works are done solely for self-benefit, they lose their true essence. Even the intention of achieving eternal life or a higher position should not be the driving force behind good works. They should naturally flow from us as a reflection of our love and faith, inspired by God's saving grace.

Ephesians 2 :10 *"For we are his workmanship, created in Christ Jesus for good works, which God prepared beforehand, that we should walk in them."*

Q : You said that you believe that Jesus is the way, not because you have faith in him but because you looked at the evidence and you came to the conclusion that based on eyewitness testimony.

A: If some one asks, why do you believe in Jesus and I say because I believe. I find that to be scary. I am scared, when I ask somebody, why do you believe whatever it is you believe and they answer me 'cause I believe. I find that embarrassing. I don't say, because I have faith. I think that's really weak and intellectually I got a real problem. Instead what I say is, I believe in Jesus because the historical evidence, not proof. I've been over backwards to distance myself from the word proof, no ! can't prove anything. Alright the historical evidence of the way he lived, he taught, died and rose from the dead, point to his trustworthiness. That's why I have taken a step of Faith.

Everybody has a worldview, meaning by that, everybody has to struggle through the questions...

- Am i worth anything or not and that's tied to where do I come from?
- Secondly is there a purpose to my life or Is life ultimately meaningless?
- Thirdly, now that I am here, how am I going to live my life ethically- cheat, steal, lie, truth, honest, we all have to make those decisions?
- Fourthly, what about after death- what happens?

Origin, Meaning, Morality and Destiny.

Okay none of us can prove anything but we all have faith that whatever we're living for is reliable. So when I say faith in Christ, I mean the evidence is, he's reliable and I choose him instead of other options.

Q: Alright but there's four things that you listed right there. What you're basically saying is that Christianity answers all those things for you in a way that is so intellectually satisfying. It's far superior to any other philosophy I've been exposed. Okay, I just wanna make sure that I get that right, so you've been telling people right yeah, to go home and read the Bible I don't know which translation .?

A: Gospels, It does not matter, as long as the translation is accurate.

Q: I assume you're out here to spread the word of salvation ? right, you're trying to get people to think the same way you do, is that correct ?

A: No, my intention isn't to persuade others to adopt my perspective; rather, I aim to introduce people to my dearest companion, Jesus Christ. Everyone asserts a truth claim. For instance, stating that two plus two equals four is a truth claim, which we can verify empirically. In every instance of adding two and two, we consistently arrive at four. Similarly, affirming that George Washington was the first president of the United States is also a truth claim. Whether we like it or not, we all assert truth claims. The crucial question then becomes: Are our beliefs aligned with reality? Jesus Christ, notably, made an extraordinary claim—he asserted to be the truth and God in human form. This is a significant truth claim that requires careful consideration.

I often encounter this line of thinking, that if you believe Jesus is the only way to God, you're labeled as arrogant, intolerant, and possibly violent. However, this perspective is quite dishonest because it generalizes and puts people in a box. Asserting that two plus two equals four isn't considered arrogant—it's simply a truth claim. Right now if you say to me two plus two equals five, that's when arrogance or humility is going to be shown, that's when tolerance or intolerance are going to be shown out . The real test of arrogance or humility, tolerance or intolerance, arises when there's a disagreement. It's how we handle disagreements that truly reveals these traits. Making a truth claim, such as Jesus being the way, the truth, and the life, or Muhammad or the avatars of Hinduism embodying truth, doesn't inherently equate to arrogance, intolerance, or violence. It's about the manner in which we respond to those who hold differing beliefs that showcases our character.

The evidence suggests that Jesus Christ is reliable in a way that other options are not. But don't just take my word for it—read the Quran, the Vedas and Upanishads, and the Gospels. Investigate for yourself and ask where the evidence leads. If you're seeking truth and want to engage with reality as a thoughtful person, seriously explore the options you consider to be good.

All I'm doing is standing here and saying that Jesus Christ is a compelling option. I can't prove it outright, but the evidence points to his reliability. You should read the Gospels directly from the source—Matthew, Mark, Luke and John. Don't just rely on my words or anyone else's.

My entire worldview is centered around Jesus Christ, so I must study and determine if he is indeed reliable. If the evidence shows otherwise, I'd be foolish for believing in him. On the other hand, if the evidence confirms his reliability, I'd be foolish for not believing in him. Therefore, it's crucial to investigate.

However, it's a mistake to think that absolute proof or evidence is required to believe something. Life doesn't work that way. We can not demand such stringent levels of evidence before we trust or make decisions. As I mentioned with the marriage example, we can not marry someone based solely on absolute proof—we also have to trust and have faith. But this doesn't mean we should be gullible or blindly trust others. We must demand evidence in certain situations, especially when it comes to matters of trust and relationships.

Q: Aren't there thousands of manuscript variants. We don't have original.

A : Yes, there are many manuscripts of the New Testament in Greek, though we don't have the original ones. However, the vast number of these manuscripts gives us a high degree of certainty that we know what was originally written. So, while it's easy to dismiss the belief in the Bible's inerrancy and mock those who hold that view, it's crucial to acknowledge the substantial extensive manuscript evidence supporting it. We have thousands upon thousands of manuscripts available for study. Come on buddy, you're playing a silly game, you can't live your life that way, it doesn't work that way. The real problem is, you're either being inconsistent or you're being a hypocrite. An intellectual hypocrite because, you're saying there's not enough evidence for me to believe in Christ but then you're going out and living for something that doesn't have anywhere near the evidence that Christ has and you're trusting it. Like all my wonderful friends who say, Stock portfolio-Wall Street, that's where it is! Man, let's make no mistake, they get up at 4:30 in the morning, they get home at 8:30 at night and they make a ton of money and that's the bottom line. Please give me your overwhelming evidence that the ultimate purpose of life is to make money. Give me a break !!, people have radical faith in the American Dream, make money. It's a worldview sir, watch out..that's pretty much it, thank you sir. Jesus Christ communicated that life is a precious gift from God.

Chapter 16

Story of our Life

Our story is about sharing a "Word in Need" for anyone going through this precious cycle of life in the most truthful and powerful way. To enable each one of us to see the value in us, perhaps not seen or understood through the lens of the reality of the 'Word of God' yet. This, sharing a word with others will enable a person to continue his journey not just through this world but till eternity, which the scripture defines as light or wisdom. Expression of this light is true Love. This love, expressed as light, is beyond our own abilities but is made possible through the guidance of the Holy Spirit within us. Today it will be us, but tomorrow we hope you will also share it with others who seek this light in a world shrouded with darkness.

It would be necessary to tell everyone concerning what my Father in heaven did for me. This is a note I wrote in 2011. At the time I wrote this below experience, please note the light or wisdom I carried was like a child. Perhaps some of you can identify with me in my particular situation. It is an honest real experience we faced together as a family. I want to give the complete glory to Him and there is no compromise on that. That's the reason it has taken sometime to pen this down. I believe it's the right time that the Holy Spirit has provoked me to do it through this book. If, I don't witness Him, the stones around will rise and speak out. The truth is, my Father in Heaven loves me..just like He loves each one of you.. There is one more prodigal added in His list. I may not be able to see Him. But He is in me. In my thoughts and as my inner voice when I seek Him.

After 38 years of being bound by his illness, the man at the Pool of Bethesda was finally healed, for 38 years the children of Israel roamed in the wilderness and finally came to the border near Canaan, known as Kadesh Barnea, just as God had promised. 38 marks the year of my salvation, healing and rebirth.

Isaiah 55:12,
"For you shall go out in joy and be led forth in peace; the
mountains and the hills before you shall break forth into singing, and all
the trees of the field shall clap their hands."

It was a pleasant day in April 2011. I had come from an US official trip back to Dubai. The trip from Atlanta to Dubai was smooth. I couldn't get any sleep on the plane, I was watching TV on the flight. I wished I had more time to watch the movie on flight. Reaching Dubai, I could not sleep for another two days. I was having a burning sensation in my chest area; was feeling very uncomfortable after reaching here. Papa and mummy were here for a few days after their trip from Israel and they were not ready for what was to follow. We spent the first few days talking about their Israel trip. Mummy joked about the food and how the people were rampaging over the Buffet, without any mercy, driven perhaps by the fear of not getting any more. It reminded me of the Israelites who collected Manna more than they needed and tried to store it for the next day. God brought down their plans of storing extra for the next day. Well I was kind of like that in my career, work, family, till this thing came in my life. It was very normal of me to get my work done quickly and on time, akin to a Martha of Bethany. I never waited for anyone, always trying to race myself ahead. I have this nature of getting things done the minute I get the job. I have my own internal panic button which rushes me to do things and oddly one may not notice it. Because I try and do it so skillfully. Well, I know it sounds like some of us. There is a time in everyone's life, that God allows you to go through a pruning experience. It is not at all easy and He will make sure that we reach a point that we learn to depend only on HIM.

Panic leads to anxiety. Anxiety leads to worry. Worry added with fear is the platform from which satan operates. Fear and anxiety are like a hand grip or a foothold, giving the evil spirit an access to influence our life. I would now resolutely say that, 'Don't allow yourself to reach that stage. Don't allow satan, to latch on to that hand grip.' In 2011, during that state of weakness, I couldn't have written anything like this. Today, it's possible for me to share these thoughts because Lord Jesus Christ has shown mercy to me, a sinner. I am cleansed by His righteousness.

Coming back to the main storyline, the dreams I had were very demonic, something like a face of a ghost similar to a black Casper emerging from the roof of a black temple. I kept thinking something or the other while sleeping; always tossing and rolling over. After a long struggle I literally dozed off due to the weariness in not getting sleep. Early morning I was feeling drained out and tensed. It seemed my heart was beating fast and I was panic struck for no reason. Fear started gripping me. I was thinking that I will never be able to sleep. I forgot the art of sleeping. This really brought me down. It was impossible for me to sleep. My head was spinning and was feeling a kind of rotation at the lower backside of my head. I was getting more conscious of myself. Back of my mind, I had a guilty conscious of all the sins in my life though I had asked forgiveness long time back. All these were tormenting me at the same time, both body and soul. I was really melting inside. My mind became very feeble and soft like butter. My chest was burning, restless and was feeling horrible. I prayed alone closing the room. I looked up and desperately pleaded God for help. I cried a lot. Asked forgiveness from the bottom of my heart and tears were falling unstoppably. My wife Sobha prayed with me. Papa also prayed with me.

Papa and myself went to see a ear specialist the following day. He gave me a tablet, usually given to patients for head spinning. Nothing much changed with the medicine, it did reduce the spinning slightly. Papa and Mummy were here on their vacation. Sobha was worried about me. I was crying loud in my room to God, to forgive me, tears came rolling like a river. The heart beat and the burn was increasing. The very next day, I received a call from my office about a high-level teleconference with a new fitness company. My GM and our Director from the principal EMEA office were scheduled to meet with the client, and my GM was eager for me to attend. However, I had to decline because I was not in a position to join them; I hadn't slept properly for the past three days and was unable to drive. They said they will sent someone to pick me. I told Sobha, Mummy and Papa about it. They said to go ahead, so that I can get away from this mood. They could already feel my situation going haywire. My parents couldn't handle the situation and they felt very weird. They felt something is wrong here. Sobha gave me the courage and God worked through her prophetically. My mind was very soft and feeble like a small child. I was crying inwardly and was sober. Papa asked me what message I received from reading the Bible that day. I shared a passage from Isaiah, which spoke of prospering in the land for many years. Papa interpreted this as a promise of richness in Christ and abundance in the Spirit.

I was the Sales manager of the company. I had a few people reporting to me. There were lot of tasks and daily challenges like any other office .

In Proverbs 29: 27, it says, "*An unjust man is an abomination to the righteous, but one whose way is straight is an abomination to the wicked.*" No one to blame as such, adversaries are part of the package. It was at the peak of my job, I had received the second best sales guy award in the group of companies, just a few weeks back before all this happened.

My colleague, came to pick me up for the meeting. He told me about his daughter who was hospitalized. I asked him about his daughter and told him that God is going to heal her. I was immersed in the Lord 24 / 7. I wanted to be something for Christ. I was deeply affected by even the smallest pain others experienced; as I mentioned, my mind was like soft butter. For instance, the sound of children shouting or crying would cause me significant distress. It was always my desire to do something for the Lord. I would easily feel sad for any small reason. My mind became so feeble. I felt an emptiness. Satan was slowly crawling in. I was like thinking very low. That's when satan tries to diminish you. I lost interest in anything. I felt useless to be precise. My mind didn't allow me to see the bright side of things. My thinking became very negative and devalued myself. I saw only the dark side of things and fear crawled in. As I mentioned earlier I was a kind of panic prone and workaholic in the milder sense. Although I was close to the Lord and did a lot of things, i had never learned to depend on him totally. I have not had any major illness, at least lets say from my 5th grade. God was very merciful to me even during the time of my reckless life at school and college. Ever since I got married, I grew closer to the Lord and was really hungry for him. I wanted to be nice and keep myself right. I have fought valiantly against various temptations from our adversary. Although I felt the remnants of those sins might be minor, I knew that in God's eyes, even the smallest sin is significant. May be I have not asked God the forgiveness of my sins in the manner He expected. God had raised me up at work in the last ten years, I'm grateful to the Lord for blessing me with Sobha as my wife. Through her, God has brought about significant changes in me.

In the meeting, they were discussing and having a teleconference. I was hearing them partly. My mind was constantly thinking about many other things. I was forcing myself to think into a Godly realm. As an effort, I was assuming in my mind that they were like Abraham and some other prophet. I wanted to keep myself thinking about God and related characters in the Bible. It made me feel secure and dependent. But I knew myself, that it was thinking out of the way. A strange feeling came to my mind, that as children how we used to have a different code language to talk to the Lord. It was a beautiful language like a nursery rhyme, and I felt that I knew it while I was a small boy. It did not seem something new. It was something which I always knew before a long time, while I was a small kid. This thought was actually a dream I had the night before. I kept thinking like this, as I wanted to pursue God so badly. It came to a point that the meeting was over. We shook hands and I commented that they had done a good job. Honestly my mind was elsewhere. I had this great passion inside me to tell about Jesus to these people. Probably by doing that, the Lord might show some kindness to me by relieving my bodily pain and anxiety !! I have a great passion in serving the Lord. I was determined to do it, I felt that it might be my last chance before death. I felt my body was decaying and was reaching death. A remorse feeling came to my mind, that my soul was at office and my body was actually kept at home. And all the people gathered at home were conducting my funeral. All of this was merely in my thoughts, which, in hindsight, I recognize as a form of satanic activity. Reflecting on my time in the US, while staying at a hotel, I read a Mormon Bible that was kept in the room.

I was seeking every possible explanation to understand my condition. At home, while Papa was asleep, he kept calling out my name in his sleep. An inner fear was overriding all my thought process. A group of people were walking outside the office, familiar faces. I went out saw them, came back telling my managers that it was the army of the Lord. They were a bit confused and realized that something was bizzare. I took that opportunity to change their attention away from business. I started talking to them about Abraham and tried to talk them about the God and Trinity. I was trying to take the example of a hen, egg as a means to explain the Trinity. It was totally unsuccessful. I was trying to tell them about God, how He came as a Son of God to this world. To observers, my actions and anxiety made me seem out of control and eccentric, a perception that I indeed embodied. I was not actually out of control, I took it as an opportunity to witness our Lord before I pass away. Principal Director stepped outside the office to inform our Managing Director—the owner of our company—about my situation. This was significant, as I had never had the opportunity to sit with our MD during all my years at the company. I took this as an opportunity to proclaim to him about the Lord. I did every thing possible to enact Jesus, how he came as a servant to wash our legs and began dancing and singing. In my mind it was my last opportunity to display my love towards the Lord. They gave me water to drink and gave me a medicine to doze off. Sobha in the meanwhile was trying for me continuously. My mobile was switched off. She was getting upset. She called my colleague. In the meanwhile our designer also joined in the office. There were a few other people, a Doctor from the pharma division. I was telling them all about Abraham, the father of believers and all related stories about how Jesus came as a Son. They thought that something was wrong with me, it was very obvious from the way I was behaving.

With much resistance I took the medicine. I didn't want to have the medicine, determined not to let it make me fall asleep or succumb to its effects. It happened likewise, I didn't sleep. They were asking me to go back home. The designer called Sobha and said that I was behaving in a strange way. The truth was that I wanted to tell the gospel to Arabs and everyone around. I was not bothered about being foolish in front of the world. The MD spoke to my wife courteously, he asked what was wrong with me and asked her whether I was seeing a psychiatrist. She got really alarmed, she requested I be sent back home immediately. They called an ambulance. I was trying to prolong my time with them in speaking about the Lord because I couldn't portray our Lord in the way I wanted. I told them that if they believe, they will see a miracle today. All of them got tired, and my GM came and talked to me very strictly that I should go back home right now. I finally gave in and obeyed him. I even tried to show them examples of how sin came into this world. As you know Muslims believe in the righteousness attained through good works of man. I was checking whether they were wearing inner white vests, as a symbolic example of being outwardly pure. Even I knew that it looked like I was being weird. But I relished those thoughts in the Lord. But unfortunately, it did not click the way I intended it to be. I didn't have the sufficient wisdom to express the message of cross to a Muslim, it was very tedious. I felt like a fool. My company, MD and GM were kind enough to handle everthing so considerately within their limits. An ambulance took me to Rashid hospital. Papa, my wife Sobha, Boban uncle(Mercy aunty's husband) and few of my colleagues came to see me at the hospital. The doctor on duty asked about the situation, so I explained what had happened and also tried to talk to him about the Lord. I was worried that the hospital staff might report the conversation to the police, as discussing Jesus in a Muslim country is generally considered inappropriate.

My desire has always been for Muslims to learn about the Lord, anticipating the day when God will raise people in the Middle East. However, my designer colleague cautioned me against discussing such topics at work or elsewhere, which instilled fear in me.

Everyone around me could tell that I was starting to panic. Started losing grip over my self. I was discharged from hospital within one hour. They checked my blood sugar, it was a bit high. Even Papa and Mummy thought that something was wrong with me, I will not blame them . Sobha was very consoling, sitting right beside, she talked to me like an angel. She was continuously talking to me from the Word. It was prophetic.

I couldn't sleep well, often lying awake until 3 o'clock in the morning. Every night, she would lay her hands on me, praying and marking my forehead with the blood of Jesus and the sign of the cross. Fear gripped me, and my body deteriorated—I lost my appetite and was anxious about work and how people perceived me as unwell. I worried about Sobha and the children. My circumstances overwhelmed me, and I couldn't control my thoughts; the anxiety was intense and unbearable. I had never felt this way before in my entire life. I realized how easily normal people could descend into madness. I felt like a washed-out piece of old rag, fearing that I would lose my sanity. Satan was tormenting my mind relentlessly. This experience made me empathize deeply with the agony of people on the streets who have lost their mental stability. I could understand their thought processes. I felt a strange sensation in the soles of my feet, my shoulders began to slump, and I was in pain. It was time for Papa and Mummy to go back, and they never fully understood the extent of my problems at that time. They needed to get to Abu Dhabi airport, so I left them at the airport office in Dubai, to catch a bus later to abudhabi. I felt tired and weary. In short, I was experiencing depression. I am proud that the Lord guided me through that wilderness experience, which led to a new birth for me and our entire family. However, I began to feel weary of myself.

We began visiting hospital after hospital, undergoing endless tests to identify my problem. It was exhausting. I continued working and managing my daily activities, but my sugar, cholesterol, triglycerides, and thyroxine levels all rose. I was desperately hoping for some medication to resolve my issues. I experienced pain under my feet, and my shoulders frequently felt fatigued. I tried to relate these symptoms to my elevated sugar levels and other deficiencies, but we could not pinpoint the exact problem.

Sandstorm Incident

We have a deep appreciation for sandstorms. Every time we witness one, we praise the Lord, as it serves as a reminder of His love. During one such storm, I experienced my head spinning while sleeping. My thyroxine levels had risen, and I was desperate to bring them down. The doctor had recommended few medicines for my overall condition. After leaving the clinic, we headed towards the pharmacy, which was only 15 meters away.

A fierce sandstorm began blowing, as if it were actively trying to stop me from moving forward. I had a strong sense, almost like an inner nudge from the Holy Spirit, that I should turn back. When we reached the pharmacy, we were told that the medicine was out of stock. Undeterred, we went to several other pharmacies that night, but none had the medication we needed. The next morning, I called Regi, a friend from my church, and gave him the name of the medication. He told me that it was typically prescribed for people with epilepsy, fits, and convulsions. He questioned why I needed it. In that moment, I realized that God was protecting me.

Later the same day, I decided to retest my thyroxine levels, and the reading had returned to normal. God had saved me from a greater danger. I shudder to think what might have happened, if I had taken that prescription tablet. Hallelujah!

I lost around 10 kg, and my tongue was constantly sticky. The state of your mind affects your body. Papa advised me not to worry about my body but to focus on my soul. I started losing my self-confidence, but I realized God's intention was to strengthen my inner self.

We frequently focus on nourishing our outer self through education, careers, wealth, food, and pleasure. However, these efforts are ultimately fleeting, as our outer self deteriorates over time. What we truly need is to nourish our inner self with His Manna—the living word.

Sobha sat with me, continuously sharing insights from the Bible, starting from Abraham. We began praying together on our knees. Remarkably, the daily Bible passages she read always seemed to address the specific issues I was facing that day. It was truly miraculous—I received the Heavenly Manna through Sobha.

We found parallels between our situation and David's, particularly when he was forced to retreat by the Philistine kings and had his wife and children taken. I was cleansed and sustained by the Word. When your situation is dire, Satan intensifies his attacks. We even lost Nethen, my younger little son, in a supermarket for half an hour. The adversary was attacking from all sides.

At work, I faced immense pressure and was demoted from my previous position. Talking about Christ at work seemed to them like blasphemy. I was anxious about the future and lost interest in myself. Satan tries to pull you apart like a prowling lion. Looking in the mirror, I felt disheartened.

However, God worked through Sobha to revive my spirit. She began speaking prophetically, which she had never done before. We also started attending family prayers every Friday at Mercy aunty's house when Papa and Mummy came. Many people prayed for me, and their support was invaluable. At work, everyone assumed I was stressed out, which was not true. They even hired someone else to take my position. I felt trapped, believing I would never overcome this. Depression hit me hard—it was a true wilderness experience. We were enduring a fiery trial, but kept receiving supernatural messages from the Lord, especially when we were broken and full of remorse. I struggled with sleep for almost a year.

In critical moments, God spoke to us through people, emails, and the Bible. At work, I was under immense pressure and felt ridiculed. Opportunists were taking advantage of the situation. My salary was reduced, and some asked how I felt about it now. I replied that they were acting this way because my God was enacting His Will in my life, and I was prepared for it. We were resolute in our determination to persevere, trusting that the Lord was our ultimate Defender..

I allowed the Lord to take control of my life, stopped thinking about myself and my situation, and desired for Christ to replace me. That was the solution. On a particularly bad day, when I thought I'd never escape this situation, Sobha gave me a verse from Psalms 27 from her Bible, providing the strength and hope I needed. Psalms 27:13, 14,GNT

"I know that I will live to see the Lord's goodness in this present life.
Trust in the Lord. Have faith, do not despair. Trust in the Lord."

The people around began speaking badly about me, spreading rumors that I was unwell and speculating that I might leave the job. I had to find sales leads on my own, just as I did ten years ago when I started as a new sales executive.

It was a struggle. By mid-2011, my sales had reached to just 2.5 million Dirhams, and I didn't receive any benefits as a sales manager that year. On top of that, I was diagnosed with diabetes and began taking medication for it. Fear gripped me fiercely, and I had never felt so weak and overwhelmed by a sense of nothingness. We began praying more fervently than ever before.

To combat my feelings of despair, I started praising the Lord loudly during my evening walks, shouting, "Praise Jehovah, Hallelujah, Thank you Jesus, Holy Spirit, Blood of Jesus." This became a daily routine, and we incorporated this praise into our prayers. We also started watching TBN channels constantly, including programs by Benny Hinn, Joyce Meyer, Joseph Prince, Reinhard Bonnke, Ravi Zacharias, Paul Crouch, Heidi Baker, Kat Kerr, Joel Osteen, Gregory Dickow, Kathryn Kuhlman, Bill Burke, Jack Coe, David Wilkerson, Kenneth Hagin, Bill Johnson, R.C. Sproul, John Piper, T.D. Jakes, Oral Roberts, A.A. Allen, and Billy Graham ministries.

I immersed myself in the Word of God 24/7, playing the Bible in my car and keeping it beside me while I slept. I had to continually challenge my depressive thoughts, speaking out against my circumstances and declaring my faith, even when my body and mind felt heavy and discouraged. We began declaring the Lord's Word over our lives, claiming all the promises in the Bible.

As a family, we became very active in visiting the sick, praying for them, and laying hands on them. We also tried to share our faith with many people, including Hindus, making use of every opportunity to witness about the Lord. I developed a passion for meeting people struggling with depression. During my visit to Kochi-Kerala, I shared my experience with my cousin Sumod, hoping to encourage him.

During our vacation in Kerala in 2011, particularly during my cousin Nithin's wedding, it was a challenging time for me. People noticed how physically weak I had become, and any comments from family and loved ones affected me deeply. Our culture can be quite direct, sometimes making absurd comments. Despite our determination to stay open- minded regardless of remarks, my fragile state of mind struggled to cope. Darkness seemed to encroach on my thoughts.

Initially, I preferred to keep to myself and avoid discussing my problems with others. However, Sobha encouraged me to confront these challenges, and we began sharing our experiences with others. Though it was painful at first, it gradually became a source of joy for us, and people could relate to their own struggles. This was a spiritual battle against dark forces, a testimony of overcoming and witnessing to others.

I gained a profound understanding of what it feels like to experience depression or stress. It's something others can't fully grasp unless they've been through it themselves. During such times, our thoughts often revolve around ourselves, fed by Satan's attempts to make us focus on our circumstances, instead of God. This is a dangerous trap.

I made a conscious effort to redirect my thoughts solely toward the Lord, although it was a struggle. Satan's tactic is to diminish and reduce us, by instilling fear. Our situations, feelings, illnesses, and hardships are all built on lies. Our thinking becomes distorted and weak. The truth is that we are like Christ in this world; we are seated with Him in heavenly places . Ephesians 2:5-7 *"Even when we were dead in trespasses, made us alive together with Christ by grace you have been saved, and raised us up together, and **made us sit together in the heavenly places in Christ Jesus**, that in the ages to come He might show the exceeding riches of His grace in His kindness toward us in Christ Jesus."*

The Word of God acts like a sharp sword, cutting through our body and soul. His Word speaks to us with piercing clarity. For instance, I felt a deep sense of dejection at the office when my junior, Cyrus, was promoted to become my manager. I had to report to the person who had been reporting to me all these years. Strangely enough, that same morning before I learned about this, the Word we received was from Isaiah: "The Lord appoints Cyrus."

Isaiah 45:1-2- *"Thus says the Lord to his anointed, to **Cyrus**, whose right hand I have grasped, to subdue nations before him and to loose the belts of kings, to open doors before him that gates may not be closed: "I will go before you and level the exalted places, I will break in pieces the doors of bronze and cut through the bars of iron."*

Then further we got this conclusion from the Lord .

Isaiah 49:25-30, *"For thus says the Lord:"Even the captives of the mighty shall be taken, and the prey of the tyrant be rescued, for I will contend with those who contend with you, and I will save your children. I will make your oppressors eat their own flesh, and they shall be drunk with their own blood as with wine. Then all flesh shall know that I am the Lord your Savior, and your Redeemer, the Mighty One of Jacob."* Whenever the word Jacob is mentioned in Bible, I take it for myself. God speaks to us in the spirit language. He tells you what is going to happen beforehand.

There was a time we cried out and wrote on the Bible, that I will be healed from diabetes. Sobha asked me to write on the Bible on which we prayed and our tears had fallen. The Word we received that day was Isaiah 43:18-21, *"Remember not the former things, nor consider the things of old. Behold, I am doing a new thing; now it springs forth, do you not perceive it? I will make a way in the wilderness and rivers in the desert. The wild beasts will honor me, the jackals and the ostriches, for I give water in the wilderness, rivers in the desert, to give drink to my chosen people, the people whom I formed for myself that they might declare my praise."*

The sales target initially set for me was 5 million, but by the end of the year 2012, the Lord blessed us abundantly, and I could achieve 10 million without any additional effort from my side. It was a clear demonstration of how the same God who provided for Elijah was also taking care of us.

Throughout this time, the Lord communicated with us through His Word constantly. Towards the end of 2012, while watching a Benny Hinn program, he spoke about a man in the Middle East being healed from diabetes. Sobha encouraged me to claim that healing for myself, and we embraced it with full faith. A week later, when the doctor performed a lipid profile and sugar test, I discovered I had been healed from high cholesterol, triglycerides, and blood sugar issues. The results were outstanding, reflecting those of a healthy young person, Hallelujah!

We shared with the doctor about the incredible work the Lord had done in my life. God has been guiding our path every single day, and we cannot move forward without

Him. My soul praises and blesses the Lord for His awesomeness. I've learned to walk closely with Him, immersing myself in Scripture daily. Occasionally, I deliver messages during our family prayer sessions, which in turn heals and uplifts me.

I vividly remember the first time I spoke at our family prayer gathering. Despite battling depression and physical discomfort, including a sticky tongue and a low mood, I made a resolute decision to speak out regardless of the challenges. It was difficult and even made me feel nauseous, but I firmly believe in the power of our words. After all, God created the world through His Word. We have the authority to declare our healing and claim our blessings. Instead of worrying about the present or future, we can command our circumstances and shape our future declaring the name above all names, Jesus Christ.

In today's world, there's an overwhelming focus on gathering information, which can be frustrating. I find myself disliking newspapers and conversations where people only trust what they see and hear.

"What eye has not seen and ear has not heard." Man looks only at the external. God is past, present and future. He is out of time and space. As Habkkuk 2:14 says: *"For the earth will be filled with the knowledge of the glory of the Lord as the waters cover the sea."*

Isn't it amazing? It's truly relieving and joyful. As salespeople, we often create graphs and set targets for the future, but the reality can be quite different. It's a profound truth that when man works, God rests, and when man rests, God works. It does not imply that we have to become lazy, but rather to understand God's role in our work life as well.

God has been performing wonders and using us for His ministry. Since 2012, I've been teaching at Sunday school, and in 2012-2014, I was leading the area prayer at our Church. Sobha had been my constant support, assisting me in all these endeavors. We now worship Him in truth and spirit, striving to be involved in the Lord's ministry at all times. This passion extends to our children as well—it's the beginning of a new life for us. Spiritually, I consider my age to be measured from the day I experienced rebirth after that incident in May 2011.

Sobha received her healing for a skin condition she had been struggling with for 17 years. Nethen was healed from his wheezing problem in 2012, and Joshua experienced a remarkable cure for his ear condition without needing surgery in 2013. His ear had an unusually narrow hole, almost like a straight line. However, God touched and widened it miraculously without any surgical intervention.

In 2008, Joshua had undergone ear surgery to remove a cyst on the side of his face, and the doctor had advised that his ear hole needed widening within 3-4 years to prevent potential problems in case of infection. We had forgotten about this advice, but the doctor reminded us during a check-up in 2012. We prayed earnestly, and by 2013, the doctor confirmed that no surgery was required for widening. Instead, he suggested reconsidering the issue when Joshua turns 15. We held firm in our belief that it would not be necessary, trusting that God has a special purpose for Joshua in his life.

Joshua often sings a particular song during critical moments, and we believe God speaks to us through him. Before his surgery, as we were heading to the hospital, he sang a song about Jericho's walls falling down when we call on the name of Jesus. God has consistently communicated with us in mysterious ways throughout our lives. We continuously seek His guidance for each step we take, and it has been the most fulfilling journey of our lives. Our conversations are centered around the Lord because that's all we know and all we love. I was working at the same company till 2022 . God had enabled us, if not I would have been kicked out in 2011 itself . God had been changing the situation gradually to fulfill His purpose. One of those days when we were fearing about our job, so much of injustice, manipulation and oppression. God gave us a verse through Sobha's mother, Ecclesiastes 5:8 *"If you see the oppression of the poor, and the violent perversion of justice and righteousness in a province, do not marvel at the matter; for high official watches over high official, and higher officials are over them."*

In my native Malayalam version, the verse comes across even more emphatically. Above my manager stood a director, but above the director stands my true owner, my King, my God. It is He who determines when my time in that company should end. Without His supreme decision, no other authority under heaven can touch or harm us.

Our identity in Christ is our cornerstone. It's crucial for every person to discover their identity in Him, as without it, life lacks an eternal purpose. Instead of fulfilling God's will, we might find ourselves constantly caught up in resolving crises and minor issues. It's disheartening to see millions unknowingly walking towards spiritual destruction, and it's a burden on God's heart.

Speaking of identity in Christ, what would you say yours is?

As per 1Corithians12:28, *"And God has appointed in the church first apostles, second prophets, third teachers, then miracles, then gifts of healing, helping, administrating, and various kinds of tongues.*

Reflecting on our walk with God since 2011, we have begun to discover our true identity. While this realization is still in its early stages, we can sense its growth day by day and earnestly pray that He fulfills His purpose through us.

During this time, we have had the opportunity to meet with Hindus and others who have faced significant hardships in their lives. We are grateful to God for making this possible. As the scripture says,*"You cannot do anything without me."* This journey is truly incredible, enriching our hearts and souls. In fact, I am now busier than ever, working at least three times as much as I did before 2011. Our focus is on saving and healing souls by sharing the experiences we have had with God.

One day, as we were praying for the anointing of the Holy Spirit, a white dove began to visit and stay on our balcony for a few days, which we found quite unusual. We needed His presence so desperately that each day became a challenge, requiring His wisdom, courage, and guidance. Psalm 107:20, *"He sent out his word and healed them, and delivered them from their destruction."*

We have been called to be stewards and ministers. If we fail to present the gospel and Jesus adequately or improperly, God will surely hold us accountable. Stewards are answerable to God.

I lost interest in watching regular TV channels or reading secular magazines—not that there is anything wrong with them. As the Word says, *"Again, the kingdom of heaven is like a merchant in search of fine pearls, who, on finding one pearl of great value, went and sold all that he had and bought it."* God is revealing His will in our lives. This journey of faith and life has made us feel more alive than ever before. Although people around us may make various comments, we remain undeterred. People at my company were slowly coming to recognize the glory of our Lord. As it says in Habakkuk 2:3,GNT, *"Put it in writing, because it is not yet time for it to come true. But the time is coming quickly, and what I show you will come true. It may seem slow in coming, but wait for it; it will certainly take place, and it will not be delayed."* We have kept this Word displayed in the same photo frame where I received my Salesman Award certificate.

As I mentioned earlier, in January 2008 there was a cyst which appeared as a small red scar below Joshua's ear on the face. Sobha's father noticed the scar and referred us to Dr.

John Panicker, an ENT specialist at Swanthanam Hospital in Trivandrum, India. The detection of this cyst was itself a miracle. At the age of four, Joshua underwent a major ear surgery where his entire external ear had to be cut. Without intervention, the cyst would have grown into his skull, requiring more severe measures, potentially including radiation. After the surgery, the doctor recommended that his ear be regularly cared for and checked again when he is older.

July 2015, our 11-year-old son Joshua needed a second surgery to widen the hole in his left ear. Although initial scans and MRIs were clear, the surgery revealed an additional cyst in his inner ear, extending the procedure from 2 to 5 hours. The doctor noted it was fortunate to find and remove the cyst before it grew further, highlighting that nothing is hidden from our Lord, who reveals hidden mysteries at the right time.

For Joshua's regular ear check-ups and monitoring, we visited Dr Hemjith at Aster Muteena in Dubai. Dr Hemjith explained that there is a tendency for the cartilage to grow back to cover the left ear hole because it had a cellular memory to do so. It meant that the cartilage was prone to regrowth due to its intrinsic cellular memory. According to the doctor, these surgical procedures were not a final solution for the issue. He specifically emphasized the word "memory" in this context. As parents, it was incredibly difficult for us to watch Joshua undergo multiple surgeries, knowing the pain and challenges he faced.

In October 2015, Joshua's external ear hole began to shrink due to the growth of ear cartilage from intrinsic cellular memory. Sobha and Joshua immediately flew back to Swanthanam Hospital in Kerala. We were praying with intense grief and pain, as the third surgery was needed to stop the cartilage growth in the external ear. His hearing was fine, with no issues in the inner ear. After the surgery, the doctor advised us to stay in India for a year for ongoing monitoring because of his serious concerns. We were warned that the ear hole shrinking could severely impact Joshua's mental health and overall well-being, potentially requiring an extended stay for monitoring, possibly for a lifetime. I was in the UAE for work, and we lacked the courage to make any decisions.

But God always speaks to his children even before any situation. In His mercy and grace, God had spoken to us even before the surgery day. On the eve of the surgery in October 2015, Sobha received a specific and amazing word from the Lord, providing us with great comfort and guidance. It is a verse that we never knew or noticed. It was Exodus 17:14

- *"Then the LORD said to Moses, "Write this as a MEMORIAL in a BOOK and recite it in the EARS of JOSHUA, that I will utterly blot out the MEMORY of Amalek(enemies) from under heaven."* It was a prophetic word which spoke to our son. 11 year old Joshua asked, how is that God could speak to me so accurately into my situation.

1. Memorial in a book.
2. Ears of Joshua.
3. Blot out the Memory of the Cartilage growth.

God gave us this word in advance to empower us to make a decision and confront what the doctor had to say. Sobha shared the message she had received the day before with the doctor, who also accepted it. When we receive His word, it is our duty to embrace and own it. We cling on to the same word until now in the midst of challenges.

Since then, Joshua has remained in good health, and no further medical intervention has been needed—no knife has touched his ear again. If we seek truth, God will generously provide it, no matter our background or beliefs. Recognizing and following the source of truth is crucial for leading a meaningful and joyful life. The confidence we gained from God's word has proven true, and Joshua continues to be fine. The enduring mercy of God has been evident throughout this journey, affirming His goodness. Challenges keep coming, but His word and presence provides us with the grace to overcome it with surety. Amen... Glory to Jesus!

God is saying to you today, you are part of my eternal story. Your life has purpose and your story matters. Walk in the direction I lead you, for I am guiding you towards a future filled with hope and promise. Trust in Me, and let my love be the foundation of your journey." - One of the daily messages sent by a close friend who is currently facing significant difficulties and challenges in life. We pray for his restoration by the time this book is released. And His testimony, I am sure, can provide many a healing.

Chapter 17

Righteousness of God

Are you hungry for God? Are you thirsty for spiritual things? Jesus said, *"Blessed are those who hunger and thirst for righteousness, for they shall be satisfied"* (Matthew 5:6). A happy person passionately desires a righteous life. It is a thirst for God himself. That is what the psalmist was describing when he said, *"As the deer pants for the flowing streams, so pants my soul for You, O God."* (Psalm 42:1)

No man is righteous in the presence of a Holy God. Righteousness is not just morality, or doing right or wrong. All righteous acts of men are like fiflthy rags, the Bible quotes. Righteousness is a quality that belongs solely to God. God' righteousness endures forever. Its about a right relationship with God.

"Faithfulness springs forth from the earth, and righteousness looks down from heaven." Psalm 85:11, NIV

In 2011, amidst a period of deep depression and a profound sense of meaninglessness, I came to recognize that I was truly an agnostic. During this time, when I felt mentally and physically constrained in every aspect of my life, I began to perceive the presence of God. My journey through this dark time lasted about a year, during which I felt ripped apart, with my health deteriorating and experiencing severe mental trauma. It was a period marked by hopelessness and a lack of direction.

However, through this ordeal, God revealed Himself to me in various ways. He communicated with me through my wife, through scripture, through the situations I faced, and through other people. He opened my eyes to my ignorance and spoke to me through my physical body and my inner being. In essence, God revealed Himself in every dimension of my being—body, soul, and spirit. He used other people and His power to make Himself known to me.

Just as Job encountered God when he was at his lowest, we can find God in our darkest hour. It became clear that God always has a plan, using every means at His disposal to reveal His presence and guide us back to Him.

Absolutely! God indeed plans to reveal Himself in His majestic brilliance, and He does so in every situation if we anticipate and have faith in His revelation. God's desire to reveal Himself stems from His nature as a revealer—it's an essential aspect of who He is. His self-revelation embodies His righteousness. God aims to manifest His righteousness in every situation. Even amidst my atheism and ignorance, I could perceive the righteousness of God and feel His glory, despite my lack of understanding. The Word became real to me in my daily life. The Word brought me the righteousness of God. It enlightened my heart with wisdom and confidence. The Word endowed me with power and healing. Through faith, the Word came into me and created in me a deep and abiding faith. Romans1:17,"*For in it the righteousness of God is revealed from faith for faith.*" God revealed Himself through the Scriptures and through daily events that consistently reaffirmed the message for that specific day.

I thanked my Lord for unveiling my ignorance and atheism. When we share the Word in faith, we're not just conveying a series of English sentences; we're imparting the Power of God through the Holy Spirit. Even the hardest heart or the most lifeless body can be transformed and brought to life. The Holy Spirit begins His work in such moments.. As Romans 8:11 says, "*If the Spirit of Him who raised Jesus from the dead dwells in you, He who raised Christ Jesus from the dead will also give life to your mortal bodies through His Spirit who dwells in you.*" Every spiritually dead person is rejuvenated into new life by the Holy Spirit. Being confident and staying true to yourself is important. And it's reassuring to remember that when you take one step, God has already taken ten steps ahead of you, guiding your path.

Due to my overpowering ignorance, I had to force myself to engage with the Word of God in a very mechanical way. Despite all the unbelief accumulated in my mind, I took the Word in blind faith. By preaching to myself, commanding myself with the Word, and being submissive to the Word, I saw my salvation. I saw my family, my children, and myself rise with healing in its wings. Light started entering my soul. Glory to God!

When cancer eats away your friends and dear ones, it causes an unexplainable mental burden and deep emotional pain. Watching a loved one battle cancer evokes a deep sense of helplessness, affecting the routine of our daily life..

Throughout history, wars and violence have claimed the lives of millions, fueled by the hidden evil within humanity, resulting in loss, pain, and bloodshed. The 21st century stands out as witnessing some of the worst bloodshed the world has ever seen.

Social injustice and inequality based on factors such as caste, creed, color, race, and wealth perpetuate cycles of hardship and despair. Terrorism associated with wealth, power, and religion has resulted in the loss of many lives. Many wars fought in the name of so called religion. Additionally, atheism has been responsible for numerous casualties in the world wars and civil conflicts, leading to a significant loss of life and peace.

Natural disasters, corruption in nature and corruption in societies, business, takes the toll of precious human life. Man is willing to go to any extend, even harming their neighbor's life, to protect their self-centered existence. Brutal murder of parents by their own children.

This generation's failure to honor mothers, sisters, and even innocent babies due to their depraved desires is prevalent. The use of poisoned substances laced with drugs and alcohol unleashes the demons within these savage individuals.

Postmodern relativists have altered the definitions of gender and sex, labeling what was once considered nonsensical as personal autonomy.

Human life has become tainted in every aspect, leading us into folly, as described in the Bible. We have lost faith in all Human systems and capacities.

In the midst of such atrocities, in a world darkened by loss, orphanhood, and marginalization, navigating through it has become an arduous struggle for survival. The **eternal word** in Heaven made the choice to descend and impart to us the message that there is a righteousness from God. This righteousness invites us into the Kingdom of His light, accepting us as His sons and daughters. It assures us that, as long as we remain connected to God and His word, we continue to bear fruit in the midst of this dark world.

Jesus says, John15: 1-4 *"I am the true vine, and My Father is the vinedresser. Every branch in Me that does not bear fruit He takes away; and every branch that bears fruit He prunes, that it may bear more fruit. You are already clean because of the word which I have spoken to you. Abide in Me, and I in you. As the branch cannot bear fruit of itself, unless it abides in the vine, neither can you, unless you abide in Me."*

John15:13-23 *"Greater love has no one than this, than to lay down one's life for his friends. You are My friends if you do whatever I command you. No longer do I call you servants, for a servant does not know what his master is doing; but I have called you friends, for all things that I heard from My Father I have made known to you. You did not choose Me, but I chose you and appointed you that you should go and bear fruit, and that your fruit should remain, that whatever you ask the Father in My name He may give you. These things I command you, that you love one another.*

"If the world hates you, you know that it hated Me before it hated you. If you were of the world, the world would love its own. Yet because you are not of the world, but I chose you out of the world, therefore the world hates you. Remember the word that I said to you, 'A servant is not greater than his master.' If they persecuted Me, they will also persecute you. If they kept My word, they will keep yours also. But all these things they will do to you for My name's sake, because they do not know Him who sent Me. If I had not come and spoken to them, they would have no sin, but now they have no excuse for their sin. He who hates Me hates My Father also."

The righteousness of God is unveiled through the Gospel, which is the Word of God. John 1:17 highlights that this Word became flesh and dwelt among us. He came to rescue us from the corruption of sin in this world and triumphed over death, redeeming us from all darkness and ushering us into the eternal kingdom. The fullness of God' righteousness was revealed through Christ Jesus, who preached mostly about God's kingdom and His righteousness. We enter this Kingdom and His Righteousness soon as we believe and accept in the one God sent as Messiah or the King of Righteousness, Lord Jesus Christ.

Isaiah prophesied about Christ, *"But He was pierced for our transgressions, He was crushed for our iniquities; The chastisement for our peace was upon Him, And by His stripes we are healed."* Isaiah53:5 As Humans we need healing, redemption and God's righteousness and this is what the world cannot provide. We are blind and deaf to what's truly important.

In the Sermon on the Mount (Mathew 5 and 6), Jesus redefined the standards of God's righteousness, marking a pivotal moment in human history. All other sermons on ethics and religion pale in comparison and are merely footnotes to the profound teachings found in the Sermon on the Mount.

"To those who pursue righteousness", *Jesus promises* **"they will be filled,"** *and the word " filled" means "sated," "slaked," "bloated," or " filled to overflowing." The metaphor expresses* *absolute and utter satisfaction: they will find a kingdom society where love, peace, justice, and holiness shape the entirety of creation."* - Scot McKnight, Sermon on the Mount

God's righteousness is not about having a holier-than-thou attitude. It's the attitude of a sinner acknowledging his sin and crying out before a Holy God. Christ saw the poor widow as righteous because she gave out of her poverty, while the rich gave out of their abundance for display. God's righteousness is distinct and vastly different from the righteousness of the world.

In His original creation before the Fall, God did not intend for man to know the difference between good and evil. Instead, as in Heaven, man was meant to be God-conscious and follow God's will. That was the standard of righteousness set for humanity. But when man sinned and fell, or could say, fell short of the glory of God, the God of **justice, righteousness and stead fast love** had to redeem man back to His righteousness and save him. The Bible depicts a loving and righteous God, who is also a just judge, working to restore His righteousness to humanity. You might ask, why did God wait so long to re-establish His righteousness? Isn't He God? Couldn't He have done it immediately? Why this course of going through an evil, sinful world with suffering ?

We can understand this, only if we understand the Holiness of our God . Holiness is something we humans cannot perceive. Its beyond our comprehension.

God's Holiness consists of :-

*Him Being Righteous King (*Melchizedek in Hebrew*),*
Him being the Right Judge,
Him being Prince of Peace,
Everlasting Loving Father,
Long suffering and Patient Redeemer, founder of salvation
Promise covenant keeper
Eternal immutable Word, Alpha and Omega, First and the Last
Has the Keys of Death and Hades
Wonderful counselor who is the Light with fullness of wisdom, understanding, knowledge, and might who dwells in an approachable light - Isaiah 9: 6-7, Hebrews 2: 10, Revelation 1:17-18 and 22:12.

The heavenly beings are so awestruck with His Holiness that they never cease to say, *"Holy, holy, holy is the Lord God Almighty, who was, and is, and is to come."*Revelation4:8.

God is unique and is beyond our full comprehension and is unlike anything else in existence. This uniqueness encompasses attributes like omnipotence, omniscience, omnipresence, and transcendence—qualities that are beyond human understanding and imagination. God possesses these unchanging attributes that consistently emanate from His essence.

A perfect, Holy God, surrounded by purifying fire, annihilates anything unholy, regardless of the degree of its impurity. Sin cannot coexist with God. His Holy justice and righteousness demands atonement for sin, meaning that sin must be met with appropriate punishment and complete eradication. The wages of sin is death, and being in the presence of a Holy God invites death.

Sufficient satisfaction or penance refers to an incomplete or imperfect act of atonement where the offended party is willing to accept it as equal, even though it falls short. For example, if someone stole $10 and repaid only $5, and the victim accepts this as adequate restitution despite it not being equal to the offense. This concept is akin to the animal sacrifices in the Old Testament for sins.

On the other hand, retribution or condign satisfaction denotes a theologically perfect act of satisfaction. It involves voluntarily undergoing a significant and burdensome act on behalf of another person, providing a complete remedy for the harm caused. This idea is exemplified in the suffering servant motif, and it's why Jesus, as God incarnate, became human—to redeem our original sin and individual sins, offering us Condign satisfaction.

God initiated a ministry centered on righteousness from the moment humanity fell from glory or succumbed to sin. Sin became an inherent condition of human existence. We witness a loving God who passionately and vigorously fights for His creation and His children. A God who made the choice to walk the same streets we tread, to face the challenges of the world as we do. Out of boundless, unconditional love, He poured out every drop of His blood for our salvation from eternal death. His name is Jesus, Yeshua in Hebrew means Lord is Salvation. He is the one about whom the prophets over 2000 years in various dispensations of time, foretold about the coming Messiah or the Christ, the Anointed One.

The reality is that many people do not fully grasp the profound truth of how authentically God has been working throughout history for the redemption of humanity. Many attempt to generalize Christ alongside all other faiths, often without making an effort to grasp the truth. I urge readers to read the four Gospels and then identify the thread that extends from Genesis to Revelation.

Here is a concise outline illustrating how God has crafted a sovereign plan from the beginning of the world for the ministry of righteousness, as depicted in the Bible. This outline traces the historical progression and the influence of sin:

1. Creation and Fall
   Creation of Humanity (Genesis 1-2): God creates humans in His image, establishing them to live in righteousness and harmony with Him.

   The Fall (Genesis 3): Adam and Eve's disobedience introduces sin into the world, breaking their relationship with God and bringing about spiritual and physical death.

2. Early Human History
   Cain and Abel (Genesis 4): The first murder highlights the deepening of sin's influence.

   The Flood (Genesis 6-9): Humanity's wickedness prompts God to cleanse the earth, sparing Noah, a righteous man, and his family.

3. Patriarchal Period
   Abrahamic Covenant (Genesis 12, 15, 17): God establishes a covenant with Abraham, promising to make him a great nation through which all nations would be blessed, despite human sinfulness.

   Isaac and Jacob: God reaffirms His promises to Isaac and Jacob, continuing the lineage through which righteousness would come.

4. Mosaic Covenant
   Exodus and the Law (Exodus 19-20): God delivers the Israelites from Egypt and gives them the Ten Commandments and other laws, to guide them in righteousness.

   Rebellion and Wilderness (Exodus - Deuteronomy): Despite receiving God's Law, the Israelites frequently rebel, demonstrating the persistent influence of sin.

5. The Judges and Kings
   Cycle of Sin and Deliverance (Judges): The Israelites repeatedly fall into sin, are oppressed, cry out to God, and are delivered by judges.

   United Kingdom (1 Samuel - 1 Kings): Kings like David strive for righteousness, but sin and its consequences remain evident (e.g., David's sin with Bathsheba).

6. Prophetic Warnings and Promises
   Prophets' Call to Righteousness: Prophets like Isaiah, Jeremiah, and Ezekiel call the people back to God's standards, warning of judgment and promising restoration.

   Exile and Return (2 Kings, Ezra, Nehemiah): Israel's and Judah's sins lead to exile, but God's promise of a remnant and return shows His commitment to righteousness.

7. New Covenant in Christ
   Jesus' Ministry (Gospels): Jesus, the promised Messiah, embodies and teaches God's righteousness, confronting sin and offering salvation.

   Atonement and Resurrection: Jesus' sacrificial death and resurrection provide the means for humanity to be reconciled to God, overcoming the power of sin.

8. The Early Church
   The Holy Spirit and the Church (Acts): The Holy Spirit empowers believers to live righteously, spreading the gospel and transforming lives.

   Pauline Epistles: Paul emphasizes righteousness through faith in Christ, contrasting the works of the flesh with the fruit of the Spirit.

9. Eschatological Fulfillment
   Final Judgment and New Creation (Revelation): The ultimate defeat of sin and establishment of God's righteous kingdom, where believers will dwell with Him forever in a new heaven and new earth.

Throughout the Bible, God's ministry of righteousness progresses from creation, through the patriarchs, the Law, the prophets, and ultimately in Christ, addressing the pervasive influence of sin. God consistently provides a way for humanity to return to righteousness, culminating in the redemptive work of Jesus and the promise of eternal life in His righteous kingdom. Salvation through Jesus may appear simplistic, yet the Grand Weaver has intricately orchestrated all of history to unfold in a way that astounds even the wise. The completed design of the exquisite fabric is a Robe of Righteousness, perfectly tailored for little children, reflecting Jesus' words: *"Let the little children come to me, and do not hinder them, for the kingdom of heaven belongs to such as these."* Matthew 19:14

I'd like to guide you through a concise overview of biblical passages that outline how God has established His righteousness throughout history. Like a flowchart, revealing the light of God's righteousness and truth.

Rebellion of man against God

Genesis Chapter 3 onwards illustrates the persistent rebellion of man against God throughout history:

Starting with Adam and Eve, Man was separated from God's presence, leading to death. This included physical death over a lifetime and immediate spiritual death, severing the connection with God when the first man Adam sinned. The inner spirit, which departs the body at physical death, was also separated from God's presence when he sinned.

Human defiance against God began in the Garden of Eden and continued to manifest fully throughout God's leadership of Israel and into the present age. Although God deemed Abraham righteous and honored him with promises for his descendants, the Israelites, like many others, rebelled and turned to idol worship, forsaking the Creator for His creation. This marked the start of idol worship within what was considered a Holy nation. Idol worship is man trying to defy God and replace Him with a convenient deity that suits the life he chooses to lead. Worshiping idols is seen as a rejection of God's uniqueness and sovereignty. This typically involves projecting human desires, fears, and values onto these idols, making them more relatable and easier to manipulate than an abstract, all-powerful God, thus aligning with personal desires and lifestyles. This can lead to a more lenient or tailored approach, a sense of control to spirituality and ethics. It often involves complex traditions, rituals, and community practices that have evolved over centuries which even can open a door to the occult and demons.

A fallen man tends to prefer rebellion, stubbornness, and an unholy life over everything a Holy God desires. The Bible describes how God's chosen people defied Him even at the pinnacle of their salvation and the fulfillment of His promises. The people of

Israel were under a theocracy, where God Himself was their King and ruler. There is an inherent natural law that governs our heart to discern right from wrong. Despite repeated warnings and punishments, the rebellion and atrocity of sin continued to increase generation after generation, revealing that the heart of man remained evil.

Moses reminds the people the reasons why God supports the descendants of Abraham and the nation of Israel inspite of their rebellion.

Deuteronomy 9: 4-8,12,24 - "*Do not say in your heart, after the Lord your God has thrust them out before you, 'It is because of my righteousness that the Lord has brought me in to possess this land,' whereas it is because of the wickedness of these nations that the Lord is driving them out before you. Not because of your righteousness or the uprightness of your heart are you going in to possess their land, but because of the wickedness of these nations the Lord your God is driving them out from before you, and that he may confirm the word that the Lord swore to your fathers, to Abraham, to Isaac, and to Jacob. "Know, therefore, that the Lord your God is not giving you this good land to possess because of your righteousness, for you are a stubborn people. Remember and do not forget how you provoked the Lord your God to wrath in the wilderness. From the day you came out of the land of Egypt until you came to this place, you have been rebellious against the Lord. Even at Horeb you provoked the Lord to wrath, and the Lord was so angry with you that he was ready to destroy you.*"

12 Then the Lord said to me, 'Arise, go down quickly from here, for your people whom you have brought from Egypt have acted corruptly. They have turned aside quickly out of the way that I commanded them; they have made themselves a metal image.

24 You have been rebellious against the Lord from the day that I knew you."

Pride Is the Greatest Problem of the Human Race

Boasting is the outward form of the inner condition of pride. Pride has been the underlying cause of all the world's evils and miseries, as detailed in Romans 1:18 - 3:20. Let's explore this directly. In Romans 1:18 Paul says, "*The wrath of God is revealed from heaven against all ungodliness and unrighteousness of men who suppress the truth in unrighteousness.*" The truth is available to all people in one way or the other, and instead of humbling ourselves under it, we stand over it and push it down. This is pride. It may take hundreds of different forms – from the most petite and delicate to the most powerful and crude – but the reality is the same: we will stand over the truth and accept what we like and suppress what we don't.

What truth do we suppress? Romans 1: 21 says, "*For although they knew God, they did not honor him as God or give thanks to him.*" The truth that pride suppresses most is that – God is greater than we are and deserves to be glorified as the supreme reality in the universe. And that God is the giver of all things and should be continually thanked. A Godward spirit of worship and gratitude is missing from most hearts because of pride. We seek admiration for ourselves rather than for God and resist being dependent on God, preferring not to rely on Him like children.

So verse 22 says, "*Claiming to be wise, they became fools.*"

This is pride. "*Claiming to be wise, [we] became fools and exchanged the glory of God.*" We foolishly believe ourselves to be wise and this reveals the depth of our pride.

Verse 25: "*They exchanged the truth of God for a lie, and worshiped and served the creature rather than the Creator.*"

Pride may still worship; it may still serve. But not God. Only a creature - something more manageable, something that can not really govern us and put us in our place.

Verse 28: "And since they did not see fit to acknowledge God."

Pride prefers not to have God in its knowledge. Pride does not like to submit to authority or depend on mercy. Therefore it is always rejecting or redefining the true God.

Due to Rebellion and Sin, God provides a written Law through Moses

Self-righteousness overruled God's righteousness, leading to a world plagued by chaos, suffering, disorder, injustice and evil. God called upon His trusted prophet and provided the Laws, including the Ten Commandments (Exodus 20) and more than 630 community and civil laws. In Deuteronomy 28, as part of this covenant, God ordained blessings for obedience and curses for disobedience.

While sin existed before the law (as seen with Adam and Eve, Cain and Abel, and others), the formal giving of the law at Mount Sinai was made explicit what was implicitly known. It provided a clear standard of righteousness and revealed the depth of human sinfulness.

Romans 5:13-14 - "*for sin indeed was in the world before the law was given, but sin is not counted where there is no law. Yet death reigned from Adam to Moses, even over those whose sinning was not like the transgression of Adam, who was a type of the one who was to come.*"

God's timing ensured that the law would be given to a people ready to form a covenant community dedicated to Him. The Law was provided to the nation of Israel. Bible emphasizes that God's choice of Israel was not based on favoritism or partiality but rather on His faithfulness to fulfill the promises made to Abraham. God's character as a promise-keeping God who chose Abraham and his descendants to fulfill His plan and purpose of establishing His righteousness.

Paul Copan's book, 'Is God a Moral monster?' Page 165... *"God was concerned about sin, not ethnicity. In fact, as we read the Old testament prophets, they (with God) were angered about Israel's disobedience, and they threatened divine judgement on Israel and Judah more often than they did on the pagan nations."* (Exodus 32: 27 and Numbers 25: 1-9)

Apostle Paul lists several works of the flesh or sinful behaviors that result from a depraved mind and a rejection of God's truth. These include wickedness, evil, greed, envy, God haters, insolent, murder, deceit, gossip, slander, arrogance, boastful, disobedience, lack of understanding fidelity, love and mercy among others. The Bible describes the fruits of the flesh in Galatians5:19-21: *"Now the works of the flesh are evident: sexual immorality, impurity, sensuality, idolatry, sorcery, enmity, strife, jealousy, fits of anger, rivalries, dissensions, divisions, envy, drunkenness, orgies, and things like these. I warn you, as I warned you before, that those who do such things will not inherit the kingdom of God."*

The law consistently portrays man as a transgressor because sin is not merely individual acts of wrongdoing, but an inherent condition of human nature.

Romans 3:20,23,NIV – *"Therefore no one will be declared righteous in God's sight by the works of the law; rather, through the law we become conscious of our sin. For all have sinned and fall short of the glory of God."*

James 2:10 *"For whoever keeps the whole law but fails in one point has become guilty of all of it."*

This verse emphasizes the idea that even a single transgression renders one guilty of violating the entire law, underscoring the inherent sinfulness of human nature. The law was always a negative marker; it never made us righteous. Instead, it highlighted our shortcomings and sinfulness. The Bible states that those who did not have God's law are, by nature, a law to themselves. The essence of the law is inscribed in their hearts, and God is a witness to their conscience.

There is No one righteous

Bible indeed emphasizes that there is **no human who is inherently righteous**. This truth humbles us and challenges our tendencies toward boasting and self-centeredness. It highlights the need for humility, grace, and reliance on God for true righteousness

Romans 3:10-11 *"As it is written: "There is **no one righteous**, not even one; there is no one who understands; there is no one who seeks God."*

Psalms 14:1-3,NIV *"The fool says in his heart, "There is no God. "They are corrupt, their deeds are vile; there is **no one who does good**. The LORD looks down from heaven on all mankind to see if there are any who understand, any who seek God. All have turned away, all have become corrupt; **there is no one who does good**, not even one."*

Isaiah 64: 6,NIV, *"All of us have become like one who is unclean, and all our **righteous acts are like filthy rags**; we all shrivel up like a leaf, and like the wind our sins sweep us away."*

Jesus says, Luke 16 :15,NIV, *"He said to them, "You are the ones who justify yourselves in the eyes of others, but God knows your hearts. **What people value highly is detestable in God's sight**."*

Human righteousness is like filthy, stained rags when compared to God's perfect righteousness. This comparison emphasizes the vast difference between the flawed goodness of humans and the absolute purity of God's righteousness. It's a stark reminder of our need for divine grace and redemption.

Three consequences persisted due to sin: -

-Man was **separated** from God, and to God you are dead.

-Our sin created a **debt** in our account with God since we became slaves to sin.

-Struggle with powers of this dark world and the spiritual forces of evil influencing our human spirit .

Isaiah 59:2,NIV, *"But your iniquities have made a **separation** between you and your God, and your sins have hidden his face from you so that he does not hear."*

Ephesians 2:12, *"Remember that you were at that time **separated** from Christ, alienated from the commonwealth of Israel and strangers to the covenants of promise, having no hope and without God in the world."*

Ephesians 2: 1-2,NCV *"In the past your **spiritual lives were dead** because of your sins and the things you did wrong against God. Yes, in the past you lived the way the world lives. You followed the **ruler of the evil powers** that are above the earth. That same spirit is now working in those who refuse to obey God."*

Acts 26:18 : *"open their eyes, so that they may turn from **darkness** to light and from the **power of Satan** to God, that they may receive forgiveness of sins and a place among those who are sanctified by faith in me."*

Picture being **seperated** from God, weighed down by a **debt** that no amount of my good deeds can repay, as even my utmost efforts are as worthless as dirty rags. Furthermore, my life is under the **control of evil forces**, suffocating me towards eternal death. This is the reality we must recognize. We are **spiritually dead**, and this is the awareness every human being needs to grasp. What an alarming situation !!! Our spirit stayed under the eternal control of the evil one, separated from God, leading us to an eternal destination, referred in the Bible as hell.

Paul puts it well, Romans 7:24 : *"Wretched man that I am! Who will deliver me from this body of death?"*

Because of the Law and as a result of sin, man was pronounced guilty. The Law could not save us because no one could meet its requirements. We were **enemies of God** ..

Nothing on this Earth or Universe could settle this enemity

No amount of animal sacrifices, idol worship, our own good deeds, donations, belief in karma, rebirth, deprivation of desires, self mutilation, adherence to cultural practices, religious practices, political ideologies, earthly kingdoms, philosophical ponderings, belief in the created Universe, self-confidence, or reliance on scientific knowledge could remove the enmity between man and a Holy God. We must first understand that nothing on earth can ever fulfill the righteousness and justice of a Holy God.

Man lives in a Physical realm with a physical Body and an inner spirit. Our bodies are tangible and visible, our inner spirit or soul is intangible and invisible. Due to corruption of sin from the beginning, our Physical flesh body decays on a daily basis and ends in physical and spiritual death. Spiritual death we read, is a separation and enemity with God. God inhabits the spiritual and physical realm as a Spirit. The Bible says Flesh and blood (physical) cannot inherit the kingdom of God. Being reborn into another physical form or body will still not qualify one to enter the Kingdom of God, as it remains in enmity with God. Obedience to the law, following any commandments, paths, rituals and performing good deeds are also insufficient to achieve reconciliation with God the Spirit. Jesus said to Nicodemus a religious teacher, *"You must be born again."* He emphasized, *"Truly, truly, I say to you, unless one is born of water and the Spirit, he cannot enter the kingdom of God."* John3:5. This means that one must experience a spiritual rebirth through God in this lifetime itself. (In general, when reading the Bible, 'Spirit' with a capital S always refers to God, while "spirit" with a lowercase 's' refers to the human spirit). Your inner spirit must be reborn as a child of God, a transformation that only God the Spirit can accomplish. It cannot be achieved through human effort. As the psalmist quotes, *"The deep calls unto the deep"*, Spirit calls upon spirit. Since nothing on earth could reconcile the enmity with God, He chose to send His own Son from Heaven to remove the barrier between God and humanity. The eternal Son of God, also known as the 'Word of God', was incarnated as the Christ or the Messiah. Christ is the second Adam who came from Heaven, came forth from the Father.

1 Corinthians15:44-49, *"If there is a natural body, there is also a spiritual body. Thus it is written, "The first man Adam became a living being"; the last Adam became a life-giving spirit. But it is not the spiritual that is first but the natural, and then the spiritual. The first man was from the earth, a man of dust; the second man is from heaven. As was the man of dust, so also are those who are of the dust, and as is the man of heaven, so also are those who are of heaven. Just as we have borne the image of the man of dust, we shall also bear the image of the man of heaven."*

Using human efforts and earthly means to reconcile with a Holy God is like trying to reach the stars with a ladder made of sand—it's fundamentally inadequate and will never bridge the gap.

Jacob's dream of a ladder in the book of Genesis in the Bible. Genesis 28:12 : *"And he dreamed, and behold, there was a ladder set up on the earth, and the top of it reached to heaven. And behold, the angels of God were ascending and descending on it."*

In the New Testament, Jesus alludes to Jacob's ladder during a chat with his disciple Nathanael. John 1:51,*"And he said to him, "Truly, truly, I say to you, you will see heaven opened, and the angels of God ascending and descending on the Son of Man."* Son of Man refers to Christ.

Spiritual death was conquered by the physical death of the One from Heaven

God reconciled the separation not when we were in good terms with Him, but while enmity still existed between us and God.

Romans 5:10 : *"For if, while we were God's enemies, we were reconciled to him through the death of his Son, how much more, having been reconciled, shall we be saved through his life!"*

Human **debt** was forgiven and **dominion of Darkness** was defeated by the cross of Christ, the one from Heaven.

Colossians2:13-15,ERV *"You were spiritually dead because of your sins and because you were not free from the power of your sinful self. But God made you alive with Christ. And God forgave all our sins. We owed a debt because we broke God's laws. That debt listed all the rules we failed to follow. **But God forgave us that debt. He took away that debt and nailed it to the cross. God defeated the spiritual rulers and powers.** With the cross God won the victory and defeated them. He showed the world that they were powerless."*

Christ is named as the second Adam. He was not sinful, but he became a sin on our behalf. As a sinless lamb he fulfilled the requirements of retribution or condign satisfaction by his life and the death on the cross.

The New covenant of the Gospel of Christ prophesied

In early 627 BC- 586 BC, Jeremiah, considered as one of the old testament Latter Prophets, had prophesied about the coming New covenant indicating a more intimate and internalized relationship with God. It also speaks of forgiveness of sins and a deeper knowledge of God among His people. The new covenant extends its inclusivity to all people across the globe.

Jeremiah 31: 33-34, *"For this is the covenant that I will make with the house of Israel after those days, declares the Lord: I will put my law within them, and I will write it on their hearts. And I will be their God, and they shall be my people. And no longer shall each one teach his neighbor and each his brother, saying, 'Know the Lord,' for they shall all know me, from the least of them to the greatest, declares the Lord. For I will forgive their iniquity, and I will remember their sin no more."*

The Mosaic law was prophesied until the time of John the Baptist, who was slightly older than Christ by a few months. The old Law was not abolished; rather, the new gospel of Christ surpassed it. Jesus said, *"People don't pour new wine into old wineskins; otherwise, the skins would burst, the wine would spill, and the skins would be ruined. Instead, they pour new wine into fresh wineskins, and both are preserved."* Mathew 9:17,NIV

143

Mathew11: 13,"*For all the Prophets and the Law prophesied until John.*"

Luke16: 16,NIV, "*The Law and the Prophets were proclaimed until John. Since that time, the good news of the kingdom of God is being preached, and everyone is forcing their way into it. It is easier for heaven and earth to disappear than for the least stroke of a pen to drop out of the Law.*"

Why then was the law given, if it was only meant to show your unrighteousness?

Rom3:19-20,NIV gives the answer, "*Now we know that whatever the law says, it says to those who are under the law, so that **every mouth may be silenced** and the **whole world held accountable to God**. Therefore no one will be declared righteous in God's sight by the works of the law; rather, through the law we **become conscious of our sin**.*"

The law serves to hold us accountable before God. This realization highlights the necessity of salvation through grace since human effort or works cannot achieve righteousness in God's eyes. Every knee has to bow and confess that we need God.

The law acted as a guardian during your early life, providing guidance and instruction, but it couldn't make people truly righteous before God. It highlighted human shortcomings and the need for a Savior. Bible says, Law was our school master until Christ came, so as to justify us through faith in Him. Christ fulfilled the law's requirements and provided the path to righteousness and salvation through His grace, sacrifice and resurrection. Just as one man's disobedience (Adam's) brought condemnation to the whole humanity, one man's obedience (Christ's) brought justification to the whole.

Galatians 3:23-25, "*Now **before faith came**, we were held captive under the law, **imprisoned until the coming faith** would be revealed. So then, the law was our guardian until Christ came, in order that we might be **justified by faith**. But now that this faith has come, we are no longer under a guardian.*"

The sacrificial system, in particular, foreshadowed Christ's ultimate sacrifice for sin. In summary, the law was given at the time of Moses to establish a clear and detailed covenant relationship between God and Israel, to reveal the extent of human sinfulness, and to **prepare the way for the coming of Christ, for the redemption of the whole world.** The promise given to Abraham that God **will bless the whole world** nations or gentiles through the nation of Israel was fulfilled in Jesus Christ.

Galatians3: 14,NIV, "*He redeemed us in order that the blessing given to Abraham might come to the Gentiles through Christ Jesus, so that by faith we might receive the promise of the Spirit.*"

John3: 16-21,NIV *"For **God so loved the world** that he gave his one and only Son, that whoever believes in him shall not perish but have eternal life. For God did not send his Son into the world to condemn the world, but to save the world through him. Whoever believes in him is not condemned, but whoever does not believe stands condemned already because they have not believed in the name of God's one and only Son. This is the verdict: Light has come into the world, but people loved darkness instead of light because their deeds were evil. Everyone who does evil hates the light, and will not come into the light for fear that their deeds will be exposed. But whoever lives by the truth comes into the light, so that it may be seen plainly that what they have done has been done in the sight of God."*

Faith arises from our heart or spirit. It involves trust in a person, not just understanding a rational law or written script. Faith is always tied to our trust, human confidence, and our essence. My faith as an human, that man can go to Mars substantiates, if i know that another man has already been to Mars. Christ has become our forerunner, who lived a perfect life, died, rose and showed us the way into the Kingdom of God. That substantiates our faith in Jesus Christ, affirming that I too can achieve it. Through faith in Christ, believers receive a righteousness that the law could never achieve on its own.

God Accomplished Our Salvation without Our Help

God has acted in history through the death of Christ to save us from the condemning effects of pride. And he has done it in such a way, as not even to involve us in the accomplishment of it. He sent Christ; he upheld his glory through Christ; he propitiated his wrath by Christ; he paid the ransom, which was Christ; and he vindicated his righteousness in Christ. And we cannot boast that we had any part in accomplishing it, because we did not have any part in accomplishing it.

In sum: 1) God's glory is upheld; 2) his wrath is propitiated; 3) the ransom is paid; 4) his righteousness is demonstrated

Seperation from God, Debt of Sin, Dominion of Darkness was replaced with Sonship with God, Imputed righteousness of God as a free gift and Heir of the Kingdom of God.

God's Righteousness, Peace and Joy was returned back to us through Christ when we received the Holy Spirit in our spirit by Faith in Jesus Christ. This is what is mentioned in Galatians 3:14.

Romans14: 17, *"For the kingdom of God is not a matter of eating and drinking, but of* ***righteousness, peace and joy in the Holy Spirit,"***

We benefit from God's Great Salvation Only by Faith in God. If you mix in works or good deeds as a means of justification, you undermine God's purpose to exclude all boasting. When boasting stops, human pride is removed..which is human effort and work to justify themselves.. There is no scope of boasting, when righteousness is imputed as a gift...

Romans 4:4-5,NKJV – *"Now to the one who works, his wage is not credited according to grace, but according to debt. Don't nullify grace and turn justification into a debt. But to the one who does not work, but believes in Him who justifies the ungodly, his faith is credited as righteousness. Trust the one who justifies the ungodly - and you will be saved."*

For God, good deeds or good works are not the root of righteousness, it is the fruit of His grace, by the Holy spirit in us. God redeems and saves us first, before we can walk in the righteousness of God. Similarly, a father first rescues his child from falling into a deep pit, so that his child could later walk rightly on a level road. Jesus came to save the spiritually dead so that we can walk in the eternal righteousness of God that He graciously grants us.

Why Christ had to die, a common question asked by other faiths ?

Clearly mentioned in Hebrews2:14-15,NIV *"Since the children have flesh and blood, he too shared in their humanity so that by his death he might break the power of him who holds the power of death—that is, the devil— and free those who all their lives were held in slavery by their fear of death."*

He had to become one among us to fulfill all unequivocal justice and righteousness of God. God cannot compromise on His own justice and righteousness against sin. So He had to die as a human itself, in flesh and blood.

Secondly, in the beginning, God foretold satan's defeat after Eve succumbed to sin in the Garden of Eden, as described in Genesis 3:15,NIV, which is often referred to as the Protoevangelium or the initial proclamation of the gospel in the Bible. God tells the serpent : *"And I will put enmity between you and the woman, and between your offspring and hers; He will crush your head, and you will strike His heel."*

This verse is God's declaration to the serpent (representing Satan) after the fall of Adam and Eve, foretelling the ultimate victory of the Messiah (offspring of the woman) over evil crushing his head. A victory over power of death and slavery over fear of death.

Why does God need to vindicate his righteousness?

The answer is in the last phrase of Rom 3: 25-26,NIV, "*God presented Christ as a sacrifice of atonement, through the shedding of his blood—to be received by faith. He did this to **demonstrate his righteousness**, because **in his divine forbearance he had left the sins committed beforehand unpunished**— he did it to **demonstrate his righteousness** at the present time, so as **to be just and the one who justifies those who have faith in Jesus**.*"

Now what do those two phrases mean?

They mean that now and for centuries God has been doing what Psalm 103:10 says, "*He does not deal with us according to our sins or repay us according to our iniquities.*" He has been overlooking thousands of sins, forgiving them and choosing not to punish. This stance by God does not seem to align well with upholding His own justice and righteousness.

King David is a good example. In 2 Samuel 12, he is confronted by the prophet Nathan. He belittled God's worth. He dishonored God's name by murder and adultery. Aaron with the men of Israel made a idol of bull, and started worshipping it. The meaning of sin is — failing to love God's glory above everything else. "*All have sinned and 'exchange' the glory of God.*"

Christ's sacrificial death also serves to uphold God's righteousness and glory. For the divine forbearance of God displayed in the past and to justify the ones who have faith in him.

The secular mindset approaches the situation differently from the Biblical mindset because it starts from a fundamentally different perspective. The secular viewpoint doesn't begin with acknowledging God's rights as the Creator — the right to uphold and reveal His infinite worth and glory. Instead, it begins with human perspectives and assumes that God will conform to our desires and rights. However, in the context of Romans, the critical question is: How has the glory of God been treated, and what is God's righteous response to that? Christ serves as our propitiation, meaning that out of love for the glory of God, He absorbs the wrath of God that was rightfully ours. This act makes it evident that when we are "*justified as a gift by His grace through the redemption in Christ Jesus"* (Romans 3:24),God will be clearly seen as just and righteous in considering us righteous when we place our trust in Jesus.

Now we are Dead to Sin, Alive to God - The Greater Glory of the New Covenant

The spiritually dead man was to be brought back into the presence of God. Recognizing one's own depravity and repenting as a sinner marks the initial step toward spiritual awakening. We are no more spiritually dead, we are alive to God. Our spirit man has risen from slumber and death and become alive in God's kingdom.

Rom 6: 7-11, *"because anyone who has died has been set free from sin. Now if we died with Christ, we believe that we will also live with him. For we know that since Christ was raised from the dead, he cannot die again; death no longer has mastery over him. **The death he died, he died to sin once for all; but the life he lives, he lives to God. In the same way, count yourselves dead to sin but alive to God in Christ Jesus.**"*

When you become alive in the Kingdom of God. God's Holy Spirt dwells within each one of us. Christ in us, so that the life of Jesus may also be revealed in our body. There is freedom in Christ, and God ordains each one of us, as His minister for the greater glory of God. The ministry of the New covenant which brought the Righteousness of God is the ministry of the Holy Spirit. This ministry possesses an eternal glory that surpasses all human imagination, extending even beyond our physical death. God brings us to dwell in His Kingdom of Heaven, where there will be no more curse. He prepares a place for us where we will see His face. There will be no more darkness in any form, and we will reign forever and ever.

2Corinthians3:6-11,NIV, *"He has made us competent as **ministers of a new covenant—** not of the letter **but of the Spirit**; for the letter kills, but the Spirit gives life. Now if the ministry that brought death, which was engraved in letters on stone, came with glory, so that the Israelites could not look steadily at the face of Moses because of its glory, transitory though it was, will not the ministry of the Spirit be even more glorious? If the ministry that brought condemnation was glorious, how much more glorious is the **ministry that brings righteousness**! For what was glorious has no glory now in comparison with the surpassing glory. And if what was transitory came with glory, how much greater is the glory of that which lasts !"*

Satan tempted Adam and Eve regarding their understanding of **God's wisdom or light** by asking, *"Did God really say, 'You must not eat from any tree in the garden'?"*

148

Satan corrupted the minds of Adam and Eve regarding **God's knowledge** by deceiving them into believing that they would not die if they ate the forbidden fruit.

Satan's temptation led to sin, which brought about self-righteousness, shame, depravity, and fear in Adam and Eve. As a result, they hid from God, and the **glory of God** departed from them.

Satan, who is the god of this age always deceives our human minds, so that we don't approve the **light, knowledge and glory** of the true God displayed in the face of Christ Jesus.

2Corinthians4:4-6,NIV, "*The god of this age has blinded the minds of unbelievers, so that they cannot see the light of the gospel that displays the glory of Christ, who is the image of God. For what we preach is not ourselves, but Jesus Christ as Lord, and ourselves as your servants for Jesus' sake. For God, who said, "Let light shine out of darkness," made his light shine in our hearts to give us the **light** of the **knowledge** of **God's glory** displayed in the face of Christ.*"

Christian soteriology includes Jesus saving us from Original Sin; Personal sin; Spiritual death; separation from God; from power of Satan, from Dominion of Darkness and Eternal death; Guilt; Shame; Law's Curse; fear of death; Condemnation; Wrath of God; Despair; Hopelessness; Moral and spiritual blindness; Self righteousness and Legalism; Idolatry; Meaninglessness and Lack of Purpose; Emotional and Psychological Scars; Fear of Judgment; Worldly influence; Sickness and infirmities; salvation of spirit, soul and body.

God's original intention for our creation was not to live with the knowledge of good and evil separated from God. Original intention was to flourish in God's presence, exercise dominion and stewardship over the earth through divine wisdom, and draw eternal nourishment from the source of life. However, when Adam and Eve disobeyed and gained access to the tree of knowledge, every human attribute began to manifest in dual forms. For instance, Love could be both good and bad; Faith could be both positive and negative fear; Respect could be either virtuous or disrespectful and shameful; Our spirt could be good or sinful. Similarly, Temper could be both constructive and destructive, Dreams could be both uplifting and troubling and Words could be both edifying and harmful. This duality extends to our Eyes, Zeal, Anger, Feelings, Thoughts, Wisdom, Justice, Morals, Truth and Desires, reflecting the complexity introduced by the knowledge of good and evil.

Our nature contains an inherent struggle between good and evil, reflecting an internal law manifesting within us. However, through Christ Jesus, the Law of the Spirit, which grants life, has freed us from the law of sin and death(old covenant). The law, being weakened by human frailty, was unable to accomplish what was needed. But God addressed this by sending His own Son in the likeness of sinful flesh as a sin offering. In doing so, He condemned sin in the flesh, so that the righteous demands of the law might be fulfilled in us, as we live not according to the evil intentions of the flesh, but according to the righteous good Spirit we inherited through Christ. He reconciled us with God and removed all condemnation.

ROMANS 8:1,10-11, "*Therefore, there is now no condemnation for those who are in Christ Jesus. 10 But if Christ is in you, then even though your body is subject to death because of sin, the Spirit gives life because of righteousness. 11 And if the Spirit of him who raised Jesus from the dead is living in you, he who raised Christ from the dead will also give life to your mortal bodies because of his Spirit who lives in you.*

Chapter 18

Jesus Rose from the Dead, So What?

The apostle Paul tells us that life from the dead began through Jesus Christ. The eyewitnesses to Jesus Christ actually spoke and behaved as if they truly believed he had physically risen from the dead following his crucifixion. If they were wrong then Christianity has been founded upon a lie. But if they were right, such a miracle would substantiate all Jesus said about God, himself, and us.

But must we take the resurrection of Jesus Christ by faith alone, or is there solid historical evidence? Several skeptics began investigations into the historical record to prove the resurrection account false. What did they discover? Some of these skeptics shifted their perspectives and became authors supporting the resurrection.

Lot of renowned Bible researchers

N.T.Wright - His book "The Resurrection of the Son of God"

Gary Habermas - "The Historical Jesus: Ancient Evidence for the Life of Christ" and "The Case for the Resurrection of Jesus" (co-authored with Michael Licona)

Michael Licona - "The Resurrection of Jesus : A New Historiographical Approach" is a significant work where Licona applies modern historiographical methods to the resurrection narratives.

William Lane Craig - "Reasonable Faith" and "The Son Rises" Wolfhart Pannenberg - "Jesus - God and Man"

Richard Bauckham - "Jesus and the Eyewitnesses"

Dale Allison - "The Resurrection of Jesus: Apologetics, Polemics, History"

My father, aged 78, passed away on September 13th, 2021, at around 8:30 pm while at home, surrounded by his wife, children, grandchildren and close relatives. He was battling motor neuron illness for three months, which confined him to his home. He faced physical challenges daily, having been a man accustomed to an active outdoor lifestyle, walking, using local buses, and dedicating himself to the Lord's ministry. As his illness progressed, his muscles began to fail him regularly, causing a decline in his physical strength and appetite over four months.

After his career as a school teacher, my father actively participated in various church activities, sharing God's word, including teaching Sunday school children and engaging primarily in pain and palliative care activities.

Its not easy to bear the loss of your dear ones, their absence creates a void which cannot be easily filled. The Bible teaches us to hold in our hearts, the belief that the day of death is more meaningful than the day of birth. It reminds us that life's meaning and value are shaped not just by our beginnings but by how we live and what we achieve throughout our journey.

Ecclesiastes 7: 1-2, *"A good name is better than precious ointment, and the day of death than the day of birth. It is better to go to the house of mourning than to go to the house of feasting, for this is the end of all mankind, and the living will lay it to heart."*

The Bible calls the death of a Christ follower as blessed. We can't take anything along with us because all physical possessions, including our own buried bodies, will stay here. The last book of the bible, Revelation, which focuses on eschatology and foretelling all future events, includes a profound verse about what we would take with us, in the life after death.

Revelation 14:13, *"And I heard a voice from heaven saying, "Write this: Blessed are the dead who die in the Lord from now on." "Blessed indeed," says the Spirit, "that they may rest from their labors, for their deeds follow them!"*

After death, our labour does not continue...its only our deeds which follow us. Revelation teaches that, what truly counts for our legacy and life after death isn't the material world we leave behind but rather the faith we hold and the actions we took. Our steadfast faith and good works in Christ will make us eligible for a rest from our labors. The good works and deeds initiated by Christ through us continue to persist into the next generation.

This profound verse reveals something crucial. As devoted fathers and mothers, the actions we undertake through the guidance of the Spirit of God are the legacy that will be carried forward by future generations. The Bible teaches that your deeds will be tested by God's purifying fire. If they fail to endure, all your efforts will be reduced to mere ashes, leaving nothing behind. Death marks the conclusion of all our endeavors, leaving no chance for further accomplishments beyond the grave.

Ecclesiastes9:5, *"For the living know that they will die, but the dead know nothing, and they have no more reward, for the memory of them is forgotten."*

This is the reality as we know, in our experience of life.

When my father and I conversed during his lifetime, we often delved into biblical discussions about death. I would remind him of the comforting truth: for those united with Christ, will not see death. John 8: 51 *"Truly, truly, I say to you, if anyone keeps my word, he will never see death."* John 11: 25-26 *"Jesus said to her, "I am the resurrection and the life. Whoever believes in me, though he die, yet shall he live, and everyone who lives and believes in me shall never die.."*

Psalmist quotes, Psalms 48: 14,NKJV, *"For this God is our God for ever and ever: he will be our guide even unto death."*

Jesus says, John 5: 24, *"Truly, truly, I say to you, whoever hears my word and believes him who sent me has eternal life. He does not come into judgment, but has passed from death to life."*

My younger brother Lloyd and our close family members were also there, observing his oxygen levels decline from 95 to 45 on the oximeter. They updated me on the situation, and I joined via video call to pray for him, expressed gratitude for his life and his role as our father. I made sure to let him know how proud we were of him. I asked if someone could read Psalms 103. Uncle Sam read it, and then Sobha, my wife read Psalms 37. Despite the challenging circumstances, I held onto hope, though there was a realization that his time was drawing near. Over the past two months, each of his bodily systems had been gradually shutting down. In his final days, he had developed a tongue infection, resulting in loss of speech just a day before. However, he continued to affirm everything we said with positive gestures and sharp responses, displaying remarkable will power and an absence of fear. Towards the end, Joshua, my elder son sang a song with his guitar. Despite usually declining to sing, he complied when Sobha asked him to sing "Hide me now" without any objection.

"Hide me now, under Your wings. Cover me, within Your mighty hand
When the oceans rise and thunders roar,
I will soar with You above the storm.
Father, You are King over the flood.
I will be still and know You are God
Find rest, Find rest, my soul
In Christ alone, know His power, in quietness and trust."
Songwriters: Reuben Timothy Morgan / Benjamin David Fielding. Still lyrics © Hillsong Publishing,

Moments after the song ended, Papa lay peacefully, his expression suggesting he was listening to us. The oximeter reading had dropped dangerously low, almost to zero, then surprisingly spiked to 75-80 just before plummeting to zero again, signaling his final moments. His serene expression remained unchanged, and none of us initially realized he had passed away; he appeared so still. Our neighbor Dr. Sajan arrived and confirmed his passing after checking his pulses and heartbeats. Mummy, still talking to him, was puzzled why he wasn't responding, unaware that he had peacefully transitioned. Neither he nor any of us experienced the typical signs of departure or the pain associated with death. Instead, God's grace facilitated his spirit's gentle departure, enveloping him in peace. – *"Truly, truly, I say to you, if anyone keeps my word, he will never see death."* John 8:51. In Christ, we are shielded from the sting of death.

The verse I frequently shared, John 11:25-26, was mentioned by the priest as the key verse during the funeral ceremony, much to my surprise. I also referenced this verse in my thanksgiving speech, and we had it engraved on my father's burial vault.

The priest offers a heartfelt invocation every Sunday at church, a Sedara prayer that reminds us of the desire for spiritual readiness while we are alive. The Priest recites, **"We, *with heartfelt prayer and plea, seek to be made worthy for a good and blessed ending, as Your promise towards the children of peace.*"** I urge readers to pray this prayer with unwavering faith, trusting that the Almighty God will grant us such a blessed end. I have witnessed it many a times, including at my father's departure.

Death should be a reminder to fulfill God's will in our lives. God has put eternity into our hearts. Ecclesiastes 3: 11, *"Also, he has put **eternity** into man's heart, yet so that he cannot find out what God has done from the beginning to the end."* This is why our hearts yearn for eternal life, and we naturally resist death.

In this life, we constantly long for eternal existence, free from the world's corruption. Yet, we often fear death and hesitate to even think about it. However, death is actually the greatest victory march in our journey with Christ. It marks a stage of elevation for

God's children, symbolizing conquest and deliverance. We understand this through Jesus' own death.

Hebrews 2: 14-15, "*Since therefore the children share in flesh and blood, he himself likewise partook of the same things, <u>that through death he might destroy the</u> <u>one who has the power</u> <u>of death, that is, the devil, and deliver all those who</u> <u>through fear of death</u> were subject to lifelong slavery.*"

Jesus has transformed the nature of death for us through His own sacrifice. Because of Him, we have overcome the power of death and the bondage of lifelong slavery due to the fear of it.

There will come a time in our lives when we feel overwhelmed and unable to handle anything more, physically exhausted and in need of complete relief and rest from daily pressures. As Ecclesiastes 12 states, all desires will cease. You will lose interest in everything, feel weak, and await death. I realize that the deepest fear we have regarding our own death and the death of others is the knowledge that **we will lose possession of our bodies and the presence** of our loved ones.

How do we then approach death ? How could we prepare ourselves for it mentally ?

Colossians 3:1–4," *If then you have been raised with Christ, seek the things that are above, where Christ is, seated at the right hand of God. Set your minds on things that are above, not on things that are on earth.* **For you have died, and your life is hidden with Christ in God. When Christ who is your life appears, then you also will appear with him in glory.**"

As Christ followers, our life will reach its true glory only when Christ appears. Our present worldly life is hidden with Christ; the life we now live is not the true fullness of life. This current existence is not our actual life. As Paul says, our life is crucified with Him. One of the greatest realities in the universe is that you (and every true believer in Christ) have passed from death to life, as stated in 1 John 3:14: "*We know that we have* **passed out of death into life***, because we love the brothers. Whoever does not love abides in death.*" When we accepted Christ, we were raised to the eternal life of God from spiritual death.

The day you were born is truly in essence, the day of your death !!! For a child of God, your most terrible experience of death is actually behind you in the past, not in the future. We were born dead in our sins. That is the spiritual death when you were born and sin started reigning your life. And your most glorious experience of life awaits you when you die physically. No matter how dreadful the suffering and death that may await you, it is nothing in comparison to what is already behind you. The spiritual death you were born into was the most perilous state, for without being raised, you would have faced the second eternal death. Thanks be to Jesus Christ, as a child of God, you have already escaped it. And no matter how ecstatic the life of this world proves to be for you, it is as nothing compared to what is hidden with Christ in God, *at whose right hand are pleasures forevermore* (Psalm 16:11).

Behind us lies the glory that our death is in the past; the worst has passed.

Our union with Christ in death took place on Good Friday. Above us and before us lies the glory that our life is completely secure with Christ in God and will eventually be revealed in all its glory. Our life now currently is hidden in Christ.

Absolutely, let us strive to reflect God's glory now. It is essential. However, imagine the defeat and hopelessness if we believed, "This is my true life: this level of holiness, this degree of purity, this depth of Godwardness, this amount of joy, this extent of glory. This is who I really am. 'No! that's not the real you.'

When Christ who is your life — the Creator of your life, the Sustainer of your life, the Redeemer of your life, the Pattern of your life, the Treasure of your life — when he appears, then, and only then, will it appear who you really are, for you will shine like the sun when you appear with him in glory (Matthew 13:43).

In Colossians 3:3, it says, "*You have died*," and in Colossians 3:1, it says, "*You have been raised*." What is it that we should strive for? We are not striving for this death; that is already in the past when we were born. We are not striving for this resurrection; that too is in the past when we received Christ. We have died; we have been raised. That is the foundation of our pursuit — not the object of our pursuit.

This is the essence of Christian endeavor: we pursue, crave, and seek after the heavenly realities because we belong there. Instead of focusing on how we die in our earthly bodies, we should seek for living out our new life raised and hidden in Christ, which is above — an eternal possession. In our journey, as we approach death, let us seek that new life. This earthly body, this temporary tent, will be taken down and removed. It's important to note that God has already prepared us for this moment. He provided us with a guarantee, an advance payment when we died and were raised with Christ the first time we believed! The order for possessing you as His own, was already confirmed, and the down payment had been made.

2Corinthians5:1-5, " *For we know that if the tent that is our earthly home is destroyed, we have a building from God, a house not made with hands, eternal in the heavens. For in this tent we groan, longing to put on our heavenly dwelling, if indeed by putting it on we may not be found naked. For while we are still in this tent, we groan, being burdened—not that we would be unclothed, but that we would be further clothed,* **so that what is mortal may be swallowed up by life.** *He who has prepared us for this very thing is God,* **who has given us the Spirit as a guarantee.**"

The mortality of our bodies will be enveloped by the eternal life of God, for which God has given us now the **Holy Spirit as a guarantee**, when we believed.

Paul says in Ephesians1:13-14,NIV, "*And you also were included in Christ when you heard the message of truth, the gospel of your salvation.* **When you believed,** *you were* **marked in him with a seal, the promised Holy Spirit, who is a deposit guaranteeing our inheritance until the redemption of those who are God's possession**—*to the praise of his glory.*"

Praise be to God, Thank you Lord Jesus, that we have been seated in heavenly places with you now, so that we have been called to reign in life..

When you heard and believed, you received the sealing at the same time, also done by God. 2Corinthians1:21,NIV, "*Now it is God who makes both us and you stand firm in Christ.* **He anointed us, set his seal of ownership on us,** *and* **put his Spirit in our hearts as a deposit, guaranteeing** *what is to come.*"

Daniel 6:17,NIV, :"*A stone was brought and placed over the mouth of the den, and the king sealed it with his own signet ring and with the rings of his nobles, so that Daniel's situation might not be changed.*"

This verse from the book of Daniel describes how King Darius sealed the den where Daniel was thrown to prevent anyone from tampering with or changing Daniel's fate. The use of the king's signet ring in sealing the den underscores the authority and finality of the king's decree regarding Daniel's punishment.

The seal we receive in Christ from God is the Holy Spirit of Promise. This promise was reiterated many times in the Old Testament. The nature of this seal is that it is irrevocable; once sealed by the Holy Spirit, we are secured in Christ. The Holy Spirit serves as the advance deposit, guaranteeing our eternal possession. When we receive this advance deposit, it confirms the order and ensures our inheritance.

Ephesians4:30 serves as a powerful reminder to not grieve the Holy Spirit of God, with whom we have been sealed for the day of redemption. This seal is a precious guarantee of our future inheritance and eternal life with God. Grieving the Holy Spirit through disobedience or sin can hinder our relationship with God and the fulfillment of His promises in our lives. It's a call to honor the seal of the Holy Spirit by living in a manner that glorifies God and reflects His character.

What does Christ' resurrection mean to us ?

Just as Christ received a heavenly body, we will also receive a heavenly body. The seal and promise of this redemption of our bodies is what the whole creation was looking forward to..

Romans8: 22-23,NIV, "*We know that the whole creation has been groaning as in the pains of childbirth right up to the present time. Not only so, but we ourselves, who have the firstfruits of the Spirit, groan inwardly as we wait eagerly for our adoption to sonship, **the redemption of our bodies**. .*"

John12:24,NIV, Jesus says, "*Very truly I tell you, unless a kernel of wheat falls to the ground and dies, it remains only a single seed. But if it dies, it produces many seeds.*"

1Corinthians15:42-44,NIV, states: "*So will it be with the resurrection of the dead. The body that is sown is perishable, it is raised imperishable; it is sown in dishonor, it is raised in glory; it is sown in weakness, it is raised in power; it is sown a natural body, it is raised a spiritual body.*"

It emphasizes the hope of resurrection and the glorious transformation that awaits believers in heaven, where they will receive their eternal, imperishable, and powerful spiritual bodies.

As per the Bible, this heavenly body will be a incorruptible, glorious, spiritual, powerful, holy body which will worship God, no more tears, in perfect harmony with the new heaven and new earth, where righteousness, joy, peace, dwells for life eternal. We have access to the tree of life for our eternal nourishment.

Chapter 19

God of the Living

The Sadducees, who do not believe in the resurrection, approached Jesus with a question to challenge Him. They referenced Moses' law that if a man dies childless, his brother must marry the widow to produce offspring. They presented a hypothetical scenario where seven brothers consecutively married the same woman, each dying without leaving children. Finally, the woman also died. They then asked Jesus, at the resurrection, whose wife she would be, since all seven had been married to her. In the below passage we see Jesus addressing the Saducees and further responding to a scribe. It was a Q and A time with Jesus

Mark12:24-27 *Jesus said to them, "Is this not the reason you are wrong, because you know neither the Scriptures nor the power of God? For when they rise from the dead, they neither marry nor are given in marriage, but are like angels in heaven. And as for the dead being raised, have you not read in the book of Moses, in the passage about the bush, how God spoke to him, saying, 'I am the God of Abraham, and the God of Isaac, and the God of Jacob'? He is not God of the dead, but of the living. You are quite wrong."*

The Great Commandment

28-34 *And one of the scribes came up and heard them disputing with one another, and seeing that he answered them well, asked him, "Which commandment is the most important of all?" Jesus answered, "The most important is, 'Hear, O Israel: The Lord our God, the Lord is one. And you shall love the Lord your God with all your heart and with all your soul and with all your mind and with all your strength.' The second is this: 'You shall love your neighbor as yourself.' There is no other commandment greater than these." And the scribe said to him, "You are right, Teacher. You have truly said that he is one, and there is no other besides him. And to love him with all the heart and with all the understanding and with all the strength, and to love one's neighbor as oneself, is much more than all whole burnt offerings* *and sacrifices." And when Jesus saw that he answered wisely, he said to him, **"You are not far from the kingdom of God."***

This is a wonderful passage, how Jesus handles the two questioners. Jesus addresses them further going into the root of those questions.

The Scribes were writers and interpreters of the Law, while the Pharisees were a strict religious sect of Jews who considered themselves righteous and looked down on others. Many Pharisees were public teachers. The Sadducees were another group of Jews, descended from the priest Zadok from the time of Solomon. They did not believe in the resurrection, angels, or spirits, strictly adhering to the laws of Moses in the Torah without belief in the supernatural. They just believed that observing the laws would give them salvation and God's favour.

Today, we can observe similarities in those who share the beliefs of the Sadducees. They acknowledge God's existence but reject the supernatural aspects of faith. It's akin to worshipping a God without power or life— believing in a deity but not fully trusting in His abilities or presence. This can lead to a kind of faith that lacks depth or vitality, as if worshipping a God without fully engaging with the aspects that make that faith transformative and powerful. It's a thought-provoking observation on how belief systems can evolve and adapt over time while still retaining certain fundamental characteristics. Even among the so called churches, who boast about heritage and experience, instead of being led by the Spirit, rely on their ability in the flesh. Even some churches, which began in the Spirit, have later switched to relying on their human capacities, having been brought up and taught in that manner. They become so judgemental and legalistic, a spirit of religion. This perspective suggests a concern that the initial spiritual intentions of these churches have been overshadowed by a reliance on human understanding and strict adherence to rules, rather than maintaining a focus on spiritual growth and grace. The word of God needs to be understood and discerned in a way that shapes our attitudes, responses, and opinions. Seeking the guidance of the Holy Spirit in interpreting and applying scripture ensures that our understanding is aligned with God's intentions rather than our own human inclinations.

Sometimes the entire preaching or teaching we get to hear nowadays, sounds like a message of hate, rather than displaying the love of Christ from the pulpit. This can create instability and confusion among the younger generation and new believers. Instead of fostering faith and understanding, it can alienate and discourage those who are just beginning their spiritual journey. For some, it becomes a platform to showcase their authority, administration and skills. Having great life experiences and receiving

God's blessings doesn't give us the right to control or manipulate others with authority. Instead, we should be led by the Spirit in humility and love, which fulfills all the laws of God.

In the passage, we observe that Sadducees response can be swayed by ignorance, fear, overconfidence, pride, and a lack of comprehension.

Jesus countered the Sadducees by replying, *"Could it be that you're mistaken because you lack knowledge of the Scriptures and the power of God?"*

He discerned their approach, realizing they leaned solely on surface-level knowledge of scripture, lacking a profound understanding of its essence.

Exodus3:6, where God reveals Himself to Moses through the burning bush and says, *"I am the God of your father, the God of Abraham, the God of Isaac, and the God of Jacob."*

We know a Moses who fled Egypt at age 40. The next 40 years he lived as a shepherd. Four long decades later, God meets Moses at a burning bush at age 80. Moses was living an ordinary, mundane life in the wilderness, to the point where he even forgot his own past.. Any dream of being used by God mightily, had already faded into oblivion. He even forgot his identity at that age. Imagine God appears to you in the faintest moment of your life, where all hopes have faded away. Moses also had this knowledge, *"The Lord is slow to anger and abounding in steadfast love, forgiving iniquity and transgression, but he will by no means clear the guilty, visiting the iniquity of the fathers on the children, to the third and the fourth generation."* Numbers14:18

He was unable to help his own people, who were now in the fourth generation after Jacob. He lived as if devoid of life, devoid of tears and emotion. If I were to hear God say, "Jerry, I am the God of your father, T.K. Jacob, the God of your grand father T.O. Oomen, and the God of your uncle T.K. Abraham," at that moment, a profound spark of life would stir within me. A dormant essence within my soul would suddenly awaken, and tears of joy would flow as I'm embraced by the timeless hope and love of God. The idea is that hearing such a direct and personal affirmation from God about one's lineage and connection to the divine can trigger a deep emotional response. It's like a sudden realization of one's significance and belonging in the grander scheme of things, leading to a surge of joy and gratitude. This is what exactly happened with Moses. Moses understood, that he was on Holy ground. Indeed, when God declared, *"I am the God of Abraham, and the God of Isaac, and the God of Jacob,"* the life and essence of God began to flow into Moses' being.

Exodus3: 2, *"And the angel of the Lord appeared unto him in a flame of fire out of the midst of a bush: and he looked, and, behold, the bush burned with fire, and the bush was not consumed."*

Moses, having heard that God is like a consuming fire, felt fear and hid his face, hesitant to look at God. However, God assures Moses that in every fiery situation in life, there is a goodness. 'Moses, your life will be surrounded by the fire of the Lord, but you won't be consumed. Just as I did for your ancestors, my life will pour into you from this holy ground. My fire will bring you life and salvation'- Moses pondered. God's voice echoed from the burning bush, and as Moses removed his sandals, the fire of God's presence filled him completely.

Moses found himself in the 'presence' on that sacred ground. We know that relationships and connections are always signs of love and affection. In this sacred moment, Moses was sanctified, and God addressed him, saying, 'Now that you are in this presence of fire, let me tell you something: 'I am the God of Abraham, and the God of Isaac, and the God of Jacob..' From the burning bush, God began pouring His love onto Moses, affirming, 'I am the God of your living fathers.' They are living even as God spoke to Moses at that instance. The life of God flowed into Moses as love, courage, and salvation.

God is not a passive observer; He is actively leading the way. He's not a spectator in the stands but is right in the arena with us. I see myself as a spectator. In the Exodus journey, we see God's people start moving their settlement only when the pillar of cloud, representing His presence, moved.

This is the God of the Bible who is living and active. He is the Shepherd of His flock. Now, it was just Moses and God amidst the fire, akin to Shadrach, Meshach, and Abednego who found themselves with the Son of God in the midst of the fiery furnace which was prepared to kill them. They were known for their faithfulness to God and their refusal to worship the golden image set up by King Nebuchadnezzar of Babylon. Our God is actively involved even in the fiery situations of our lives. His Word is live and active, that it can go deep and discern the thoughts, intentions and plight of our spirit, soul and body. We have a God, who is actively involved in our life and relationships.

Jesus was essentially pointing out to the Sadducees that the scriptures they claimed to know so well, actually spoke directly to their most revered prophet, Moses, specifically about their own forefathers, indicating that they were still alive in God's eyes.

Do we believe in the God of the dead or the God of the living? Believing in the God of the living means that His fire doesn't consume us; instead, it sanctifies us. We are never alone anymore; we walk alongside God, who then becomes our guide. Yet at times, we act like the Sadducees, behaving as if God isn't alive. Understanding the life of God within us, frees us from all bondage and fills us with His wisdom to handle any existential questions we face.

There is a song which goes like this:

O, Man ! there is no need to be fearful henceforth
on your journey towards Zion.
The God of Abraham, The God of Issac
The God of Jacob is always with you.

Even though in the eyes of the world,
i might look like a fool.
Yet I will be always exalted
in the eyes of God.
The God of Abraham,The God of Issac
The God of Jacob is always with you.

For sure, i do not need henceforth
the trust of the world.
Trust in God,
thats the only one thing for me.
The God of Abraham,The God of Issac
The God of Jacob is always with you.

I do not worry
about anything.
The one who gave me the life giving Bread
will lead me abundantly till eternity.
The God of Abraham,The God of Issac
The God of Jacob is always with you.

In the second part of the Mark's passage, Jesus responded to a deep probing question from a Scribe about the most important commandment among all the multitude of 630 commandments and laws which they needed to learn and practice on a daily basis. Here one of the scribes, who was at that time, a very respectable, dignified personality in the Jewish community seeing that Jesus replied well, he wanted to clear certain uncertainities of his profession.

Whenever we reach a point in life filled with uncertainty and sorrow, we often ask many deep, probing questions. Responses like, "Why has this happened to me?" or "Why me?" are common. If we analyze these truth questions, we find that each one carries an underlying intention. On the surface, they might seem like simple inquiries, much like those asked by a scribe. However, they often reflect a deeper search for meaning, understanding and connection. At a basic level, people want to make sense of their experiences. Understanding the reasons behind suffering can provide a sense of order and meaning in a chaotic situation. It's a way to vocalize the internal turmoil and seek empathy or validation from others.

When faced with uncertainty, people may look for reasons to regain a sense of control. If they can pinpoint why something happened, they might believe they can prevent it in the future or handle it better. The surface question is often just a doorway to deeper emotional and psychological landscapes. Understanding this can foster more empathetic and supportive responses, whether we are addressing our own questions or those of others.

We live in a world where we encounter numerous questions from various people. On the surface, these questions may seem like simple inquiries.

However, it is essential to respond by understanding the deeper root of these questions or interactions.

The crack in your ceiling may not always align directly above it; it could be the result of a fracture running through the concrete, only appearing at a different spot on the roof. This serves as an analogy for how the root of any surface issue can manifest elsewhere. The questions, issues, and cracks others might have at the surface level of their lives are often rooted in a different, deeper existential place within their understanding.

God's Spirit and His word can discern those deeper places of human mind.

If we delve deeply into the root of any question, it fundamentally touches on the four basic aspects of our existence that we constantly ponder as human beings:

Where did I come from ?

What kind or quality of life am I meant to live ?

What is the meaning and purpose of my existence ?

Where do I end up eventually ?

In short, its about Origin, Morality, Meaning and Destiny of Life. Always recognize that any serious question about life being asked of you likely encompasses these four fundamental elements.

The scribe queried Jesus, "Which commandment holds the utmost importance?" Scribes, whose main task involves copying scriptures onto scrolls and teaching their principles, undoubtedly posed a question closely tied to his own livelihood—a pivotal inquiry for their flourishing. It was key to his thriving as a teacher and writer in his community.

Observe how Jesus responds to the question. True to form, he references the scripture known as the Shema of Israel, a creed or song recited by every Jew. Shema Yisrael, or the Shema, is the central affirmation of Judaism from Deuteronomy 6. The prayer expresses belief in the singularity of God, that is, in God's oneness and incomparability.

"Shema yisrael Adonai eloheinu Adonai echad. [Response:- barukh shem kevod malkhuto le'olam va'ed. blessed is the name of His glorious kingdom forever and ever] Ve'ahavta et Adonai eloheykha bekhol-levavkha u'vekhol nafshekha u'vekhol me'odekha.)" - Deuteronomy 6: 4

"Hear, O Israel: The Lord our God, the Lord is one. And you shall love the Lord your God with all your heart and with all your soul and with all your mind and with all your strength.' The second is this: 'You shall love your neighbor as yourself."- Mark12: 29-31

Jesus starts, "Hear, O Israel: The Lord our God, the Lord is one," is the answer to the deep-rooted question, **Where do I come from ?, ORIGIN** — The Shema declares that God is the **One** for everything in your life; we come from God. In verse 32, the scribe responds to Jesus, *"You are right, Teacher. You have truly said that he is one, and there is no other besides him."* Jesus addresses the origin question by emphasizing the importance of listening: *"Hear, O Israel, the Lord our God, the Lord is one."* This means that for any questions in life, we must understand that all answers are found in God. The One who is the answer to all our questions is God. One also emphasizes that there is none like Him, for He is unique in His essence, power, and attributes.. The scribe might have felt a profound sense of awe, reverence, and humility upon hearing this statement. It sparked a realization of God's unparalleled greatness and uniqueness, deepening his faith and confidence in his calling to write the scripture. When we explain to others that everything in this world originates from God, we address the foundational answer to at least 1 out of 4 of their problems and questions. Lamentations 3: 37, *"Who has spoken and it came to pass, unless the Lord has commanded it?"* Introducing God into your interactions primarily opens a window of hope and light into the heart and mind of the listener. That's the void which can be only filled by God. That resolves a lot of questions and instabilities.

What kind or quality of life am I meant to live? Furthermore, the Shema teaches that the highest and most complete form of **Morality** is to **love God and love others**. The weight of upholding all these laws was an overwhelming burden and an existential challenge to practice it. Jesus was subtly teaching that love is the only way to truly fulfill God's commandment—there is no other way to achieve it. When Jesus unveiled the true meaning of the scriptures, revealing that all the laws were ultimately pointing towards God's love, the scribe felt both relieved and enlightened. As Galatians 5:14 states, *"For the whole law is fulfilled in one word: "You shall love your neighbor as yourself."* This realization gave the Scribe a profound understanding of the quality of life that the laws aim to promote. Despite his community's rigorous tradition of strictly obeying all 630 laws, he came to understand that there is something greater—loving God and loving others.

Love is the ultimate moral value and the highest wisdom we must embody, love transcends all laws. 1Peter4:8 *"Above all, love each other deeply, because love covers over a multitude of sins."* When we love God and love others, all barriers and evil desires of the flesh are overcome. After a child is introduced to God, an ideal parent should guide the child to understand the fundamental nature of God—that God is love.

1John4: 7-12, *"Beloved, let us love one another, for love is from God, and whoever loves has been born of God and knows God. Anyone who does not love does not know God, because God is love. In this the love of God was made manifest among us, that God sent his only Son into the world, so that we might live through him. In this is love, not that we have loved God but that he loved us and sent his Son to be the propitiation for our sins. Beloved, if God so loved us, we also ought to love one another. No one has ever seen God; if we love one another, God abides in us and his love is perfected in us."*

God loves us not because primarily we are loveable but because He is love. God's purpose of Love was there before creation. Our idea about God's Love has lot of false assumptions. The Love we try to define is only the shadow of the real one. A selfless love which pursues man… Our love is generally and mostly conditional.

All names in heaven and earth are established and written by God only when we are rooted and grounded in this same love of God. God's name has an identity embedded in Love. Paul prays for the same depth of Love in us. Paul prays earnestly for a power in our inner being from God's spirit, so that we may walk in the fullness or completeness of God's love.

Ephesians3:14-19, "*For this reason I kneel before the Father, from whom every family in heaven and on earth derives its name.(further in verse he continues)...I pray that out of his glorious riches he may **strengthen you with power through his Spirit in your inner being**, so that Christ may dwell in your hearts through faith. And I pray that you, being **rooted and established in love**, may have power, together with all the Lord's holy people, to grasp how **wide and long and high and deep is the love of Christ**, and to know this love that surpasses knowledge—that you may be filled to the measure of all the fullness of God.*"

God's love is an expression of His heart, understood by our inner self. Fully understanding His love is as challenging as understanding God. The verse describes this love as surpassing knowledge. Comprehending it fully is a lifelong endeavor. Paul tells the Ephesians that this love must be complete, filled with all the fullness of God. Praying in this way allows Christ to dwell within us. We need God's power to truly understand and love Him.

Whats the meaning and purpose of my being? After receiving answers from Jesus revealing his origin and morality, the scribe experiences a surprising shift as he discovers newfound meaning and purpose in his life, prompting a heartfelt response., Mark12:33, "*And to **love Him** with all the heart and with all the understanding and with all the strength, and to love one's neighbor as oneself, **is much more than all whole burnt offerings and sacrifices.**"*

Filled with a sense of meaning and purpose, the Scribe realizes the importance of loving God with all aspects of his being—spirit, soul, and body. Previously accustomed to the routine practices of sacrifices and burnt offerings as a scribe, he found no meaningful connection to his life in those rituals. The endless cycles of animal sacrifices and offerings had become a meaningless and exhausting routine in his life, where everything appeared to be a relentless cycle of bloodshed. Our daily mechanical routines can become tiresome, and we may perceive them as lacking meaning. We worry and get negative. However, when we grasp the notion that everything is ordained by God and then structure our lives and relationships around this sacred principle of life, which involves loving God and serving humanity, we find a profound sense of purpose and fulfillment. Our work, relationships, preferences, and entire existence gain deep meaning and significance when God's love is at the core of everything, serving as the driving force for our actions and intentions.

Where do I end up eventually ? Our destiny, Finally Jesus quotes his DESTINY--Mark12: 34, *"And when Jesus saw that he answered wisely, he said to him, "You are not far from the **kingdom of God**."* His Destiny is an eternal life in the Kingdom of God. God extends to us the gift of eternal life, revealing the depth of His eternal love for us through our faith in Jesus Christ our redeemer. The Scribe finds his joy, destiny and redemption, that God provides. God has prepared a place for us in His Kingdom

There's profound impact when we share the love of God with hurting people; it gives them a sense of purpose and significance and brings meaning and hope to our own lives. Moses, for instance, experienced such transformation at age 80, forgetting his origin, meaning, morality and destiny until he encountered God. To grasp God's love, we must first appreciate the precious gift of life given to us, sustained daily until eternity. Recognizing **life as a blessing from God** can profoundly change our perspective. We sometimes connect our mechanical work with our life. These are two different aspects. Your work should not affect your life. Life is a precious gift from God, it is given to you by God for loving Him and loving others. Work can be likened to the curry, while life is like the main bread. Just as we store them separately in containers in a refrigerator to maintain their freshness, it's crucial to keep our profession and life distinct. Mixing them can lead to a negative impact on our mental and emotional well-being, akin to spoiling the taste of our food, when we try to mix and store the curry and bread in a single container. Understanding that we serve a living God who is sovereign and actively involved in our world allows us to comprehend the worries and questions of our lives, much like the scribe did. In our interactions with people facing burdens and questions, if we can illuminate these four existential aspects of life for them, they will begin to connect with their own experiences.

The Living God who flows out of you – the fountain

The love of God through the Holy Spirit is a genuine experience that comes with faith in Christ. This supernatural work of the Holy Spirit cannot be achieved by human effort; it is a miracle for all of broken humanity. It is not dependent on our goodness, family background, heredity or religion. Every follower of Christ has encountered the love of the Holy Spirit, which defies logic because the full comprehension of God's love is beyond us, as stated in Ephesians 3:18. This is evident in Christ's interactions with many, such as the Samaritan woman at Jacob's well and others in the New Testament. As we journey with the Holy Spirit, God's love, poured into us by His Spirit, flows through us like rivers of love, overflowing as living water from our hearts to touch the lives of others.

Christ assures us that He is preparing a place for those who accept His truth and follow His commands. As He says in John 14:1-3, *"Let not your hearts be troubled. Believe in God; believe also in me. In my Father's house are many rooms. If it were not so, would I have told you that I go to prepare a place for you? And if I go and prepare a place for you, I will come again and will take you to myself, that where I am you may be also."*

Why would a man, aware that He is to be crucified by His own brothers, console us and assure us that nothing in this world can trouble us? He lovingly commands us, warning us not to let our hearts be troubled in any way. The promise of eternal companionship and a prepared place, particularly coming from someone on the brink of death, is remarkable for how it provides reassurance and fosters our trust in Jesus. Jesus offers a larger, loving plan with no expectation of personal gain.

Jeremiah prophesied, *"For My people have committed two evils: They have forsaken Me, The fountain of living waters, To hew for themselves cisterns, broken cisterns that can hold no water."* Jeremiah 2:13

Are we carrying broken cisterns that can hold no water? God, through Christ Jesus, offers us healing and an unbreakable cistern, an indestructible life in Him. The question remains: have we received Him? Is your jar filled with the water of eternal life? Each heartbeat reminds us that time is fleeting. God has prepared a Fountain of Life without barriers; all we need to do is open our hearts, remove all veils, and pray with childlike innocence, 'God, if you are real, please reveal your glory to me and show me the path to your life.' For us to say this simple prayer, our loving God orchestrated history, paying a great price and enduring much to make this possible. The pursuing love of God is the greatest wonder in the spiritual universe... when we see these glimpses of God's love at work from the beginning...in the lives of Abraham, Moses, David, Daniel, Hosea, the prophets till John the Baptist, we may wonder if God is really like that., Gods love is an eternal love which seeks the lost and is an identity of who God is.

Every believer of Christ, is promised a comforter, the Holy Spirit. The Holy Spirit pours out God's love in us and in return we experience the true love of God. We can feel the love of God in our daily life and this love flows from us seeking to love the people around us. We strive to share the love of God that we have received with others. Many interpret this sharing, as Christians trying to convert religions, that's not true. It's the overflowing love of God permeating from our being. God gives us His Spirit to love others, its infectious. His love produces eternal Hope in us. It bubbles inside us like a fountain, kept alive by His Word and His Spirit. God becomes so real to us than even other human beings. He gives us what we need, through His Word and through the Holy spirit. Only a true Christ follower can understand this, others may wrongly define it as practicing religion.

His love restores and renews, allowing us to see our lives through a new lens, filled with the newness of life we've received from God. We begin to see everyone as a precious creation of God. There is no competition or performance in God's kingdom to prove our worth. The race was already won and death was conquered by the leader of our faith, Christ Jesus Himself. Christ places us in Heaven when we put our faith in Him, then we begin a new life as a heavenly citizen, embraced by love, hope, and faith. This isn't theoretical knowledge; it's a real thing you experience as a believer. All bondages, burdens and afflictions then starts to give meaning and purpose in life and you know that God will change it for good. You never will again try to display or keep an account of your own self righteousness or good works, since you are overshadowed by the Righteousness of a Loving heavenly Father. Because everything comes out of your being through God's love in you.

Don't forget, we are living in an era where transhuman hackers are implanting chips in their bodies, and we are surrounded by deception and virtual realities. The future will likely be shaped by a complex interplay of technological innovations, ethical considerations and societal responses. While technology offers immense potential benefits, it also poses significant challenges. Human life will face new threats when technology is used for malicious purposes, such as cyber attacks, unauthorized surveillance, or the creation of weapons of mass destruction, potentially causing significant harm. Love comes from God but strife and destruction comes from the enemy of our soul. But God's passionate love can overshadow anything which comes against a believer.

Let us go through the Bible portion Romans 8:31-35,37-39, about God's Everlasting Love, "*What then shall we say to these things? If God is for us, who can be against us? He who did not spare his own Son but gave him up for us all, how will he not also with him graciously give us all things? Who shall bring any charge against God's elect? It is God who justifies. Who is to condemn? Christ Jesus is the one who died—more than that, who was raised—who is at the right hand of God, who indeed is interceding for us. Who shall separate us from the love of Christ? Shall tribulation, or distress, or persecution, or famine, or nakedness, or danger, or sword? No, in all these things we are more than conquerors through Him who loved us. For I am sure that neither death nor life, nor angels nor rulers, nor things present nor things to come, nor powers, nor height nor depth, nor anything else in all creation, will be able to separate us from the love of God in Christ Jesus our Lord."*

Paul describes God's passionate love through the best vocabulary of words he could. Paul perhaps in this scientific age would have quoted….. 'No Time, space and matter can separate us from such a Great Love.' Romans 8:32 reveals God's profound love by showing that He sacrificed His own Son to save us. This act of immense sacrifice demonstrates the depth of His compassion and goodness. If God can overcome such a significant obstacle, Paul argues that God can easily address any other needs we may have. This illustrates the boundless grace of a loving Father who will also care for our needs in body, mind, and spirit.

If we truly reflect and experience God's love, it has to naturally overflow into our interactions with others. The Holy Spirit, given to us through Christ, is a gift of God's love that enables us to love others and spread that love. This divine love fosters eternal hope within us. Like a lover boy, our God also wants to share His Delights with us .

Isaiah 62: 4,NIV, *"No longer will they call you Deserted, or name your land Desolate. But you will be called Hephzibah (means My delight Is in Her), and your land Beulah (means Married) :for the LORD will take delight in you, and your land will be married."*

Jesus described Himself as the bridegroom and believers as His betrothed bride. The final book of the Bible describes the marriage supper of the Lamb, where Christ, the bridegroom, will welcome His beautifully adorned bride(Church of believers)dressed in garments of salvation and robes of righteousness (Isaiah 61:10). This event is not a literal marriage but symbolizes a holy spiritual, covenantal relationship with God. The Holy Spirit is given to us as believers now, as a seal of His ownership and a sign of God's passionate love, serving as a deposit for the upcoming final wedding ceremony, the marriage supper of the Lamb. How amazing is that*!*

Revelation 19: 6-8,NIV, "Then I heard what sounded like a great multitude, like the roar of rushing waters and like loud peals of thunder, shouting: "Hallelujah! For our Lord God Almighty reigns. Let us rejoice and be glad and give him glory! For the wedding of the Lamb has come, and his bride has made herself ready. Fine linen, bright and clean, was given her to wear." (Fine linen stands for the righteous acts of God's holy people.)

Jesus stands as an eternal fountain of the water of life, inviting us to come closer. As we approach this divine source of fountain, we are enveloped by the Grace of God. A Grace flows into us, assuring that even in times of being bedridden or broken, our present afflictions are but temporary and we proclaim that these sufferings will be far surpassed by His eternal glory reserved for us. A Grace that resolutely declares, "I will not bow down to anything else, regardless of whether I emerge from the fiery furnace alive or dead." A Grace that grants peace and forgiveness even as my hands and feet are nailed to a wooden cross. A Grace that extends love and compassion to every person, regardless of their background, color, religion, or any other worldly distinctions. A Grace that, despite every thorn in the flesh, amidst ashes and sores, and in the face of all opposing forces—when we have lost everything and are weary from life—proclaims, "I will live to witness His glory in this very life." A Grace that thrives within me like an invincible fountain, even in the face of insults, brutality, slander, strikes, and false accusations. A Grace that shuts the mouths of lions when we are cast into their den, providing protection and peace amid the threat of danger. A Grace that clings tenaciously to the frail leaf of faith, even when hope appears utterly obliterated, when those around you turn their backs, and you are burdened by the weight of being the most despicable sinner. A Grace that boldly declares, "My God will provide" even as I confront death and desolation. A Grace that can discern with unwavering clarity and certainty, the voice of the Great Shepherd above all other voices, including voices of my own doubts and the wisdom of the world. A Grace that fully embraces the testimony of Jesus without shame, willingly sharing in the suffering it entails, as I am called to a holy life with God —one that has conquered death and revealed life and immortality through the gospel. A Grace that reveals to me that God is my Father, and allows me to call Him "Abba, Father," bestows upon me a sound mind and directs me to reflect His love to others. The Grace and love of a father who cherishes his son, understanding me more deeply than I understand myself, filling every gap in my soul and moulding me into a better version of myself, and constantly reminding me of my inherent value. A Grace which assures me that even through life's storms, deprivations, and death, I am continually progressing toward ultimate glorification. A Grace that does not put me in shame, but will have sufficient courage, so that now as always, Christ will be exalted in my body, whether by life or by death. For to me, to live is Christ and to die is gain. A Grace that, when I am thirsty, empowers me to approach God with boldness at His throne of grace whenever I wish, and to receive the Fountain of living water at no cost from the One Who was, Who is, and Who is to come. Amen, Amen, Amen.

Revelation 21: 5-8, *NIV, "He who was seated on the throne said, "I am making everything new!" Then he said, "Write this down, for these words are trustworthy and true." He said to me: "It is done. I am the Alpha and the Omega, the Beginning and the End. To the thirsty I will give water without cost from the Fountain of the water of life. Those who are victorious will inherit all this, and I will be their God and they will be my children. But the cowardly, the unbelieving, the vile, the murderers, the sexually immoral, those who practice magic arts, the idolaters and all liars—they will be consigned to the fiery lake of burning sulfur. This is the second death."*

In a world that's racing ahead with technological marvels and constant progress, it's admirable to see how we push ourselves to improve and innovate. We rightly value hard work and dedication.

Yet, despite our achievements, there's a deep-seated need for a guiding **Light—a source of true wisdom** to help us navigate our everyday lives. When the wisdom we seek is not anchored in a solid foundation, especially when we face death or existential peril, all our achievements and our truths may ultimately dissolve into vanity and meaninglessness.

We are driven to pursue authority and **glory**, yearning to control our environment and shape our destinies. Yet, human history stands as a testament to the inevitable decline of every empire and ruler as time marches on. The relentless ticking of the clock reveals the transient nature of power and the impermanence of greatness.

This relentless pursuit of **knowledge,** a deeper understanding of the world and staying informed can sometimes feel overwhelming. While seeking knowledge is valuable, it can also bring sorrow by increasing awareness of life's uncertainties. This paradox highlights the fragile nature of human endeavors for light, knowledge and glory when divorced from a deeper, enduring truth. Paul the Apostle boldly proclaims to the diverse and sophisticated citizens of ancient cosmopolitan city of Corinth—comprising of searchers of Light, pursuers of Knowledge, seekers of Glory and lovers of pleasure- *"That the same God who commanded, "Let light shine out of darkness," made his light shine in our hearts to give us the **light** of the **knowledge of God's glory** displayed in the face of **Christ**."*- 2 CORINITHIANS 4:6

We find our true origin, meaning, morality and destiny when we receive the fountain of truth in Christ Jesus. Many people often turn to accept the truth and seek God only when the smell of death strikes their mind and body. However, it is important not to wait until it is too late to embrace salvation. Today, if you hear His call, do not harden your heart. Your inner spirit yearns for redemption and fulfillment. Surrender your precious life to Jesus Christ, the great fountain of life.

Faith is the realization of my sinfulness, where I hear God's voice and see His boundless love in the blood-stained wounds of Jesus which calls to embrace me as His beloved child empowering me to overcome the world not through fear or my own strength but with the serene confidence of a child who knows his Father is always near.

You are valuable and precious my Friend. He provides the seed for the sower and bread for the eater.

"A truly Christian love, either to God or men, is a humble broken-hearted love. The desires of the saints, however earnest, are humble desires. Their hope is a humble hope; and their joy, even when it is unspeakable and full of glory, is a humble broken-hearted joy, and leaves the Christian more poor in spirit, and more like a little child, and more disposed to a universal lowliness of behaviour."
— Jonathan Edwards, The Religious Affections

About the Author

I'm Jerry Jacob, a 51-year-old from Kerala, India, now living in Dubai. After completing my engineering education in Kerala, I moved to Bombay in 1995 to find work. With a career primarily in sales, I currently work with a health and fitness company at Dubai. Christ is central to my identity, and I'm passionate about theology and sharing wisdom to uplift others.

Living in Dubai, a melting pot of cultures, enriches my personal and professional life, allowing me to build meaningful connections and discover my identity. I focus on shared values rather than differences, viewing my presence here as a testament to God's guidance in serving His purpose. Sobha and I are blessed with two wonderful children, Joshua and Nethen, who provide strength and support as we navigate life together. We believe in valuing all individuals, recognizing that everyone is created in the image of God.

The hand of God has been evident at every stage of my life as I sought His reality. "Seed for the Sower and Bread for the Eater" is my humble attempt to share the goodness we've received, inspired by Christ's love. As a weak vessel, I hope to enlighten readers through my weaknesses, embodying the truth that 'light flows out of darkness.' While my writing skills are average, I believe the truth of Christ can satisfy every thirsty soul. This book addresses spiritual and existential questions simply for agnostics, believers, and truth-seekers. My passion for writing on spiritual themes began in school, focusing on profound truths from a common perspective. Since 2011, I've shared insights on my website, www.wordinneed.com, and through occasional audio podcasts.

As a family, we love sharing the word of God, whether with church prayer groups, friends from school and college, or individuals from various nationalities. We strive to offer spiritual support to those in difficult times and are committed to teaching Sunday school. Love to witness Christ to people from different backgrounds and religions, and are passionate about praying for the sick and engaging with those who are depressed.

A few years ago, I dedicated myself to learning Old Biblical Hebrew to deepen my understanding of the Biblical context. My commitment is to make challenging ideas accessible and engaging, bridging gaps for truth-seekers with insights that resonate in both heart and mind, guided by the Holy Spirit. My journey to fill the voids and darkness within my heart—shaped by personal struggles—is fueled by God, who continually helps us recognize the gaps in our lives.

Printed in the United States
by Baker & Taylor Publisher Services